Interior Design-Furnishings Directory of Discounted 800-Number and Hard-to-Find Companies

Including
North Carolina
Furniture
Sources!

Insider's Home Decorating Directory of Lower-Priced and Little-Known Companies that Offer You Substantial Savings and Higher Values

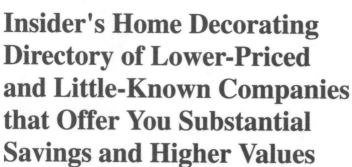

Touch of Design ®

Interior Design Furnishings Directory of Discounted 800-Number and Hard-to-Find Companies

Including North Carolina Furniture Sources!

Insider's Home Decorating Directory of Lower-Priced and Little-Known Companies that Offer You Substantial Savings and Higher Values

Touch of Design ®

Interior Design-Furnishings Directory of Discounted 800-Number and Hard-to-Find Companies

Insider's Home Decorating Guide of Lower-Priced and Little-Known Sources that Offer You Substantial Savings and Higher Values

By Linda M. Ramsay

Published by:

Touch of Design®

475 College Boulevard, Suite 6290
Oceanside, California 92057 U.S.A.
(619) 945-7909
todesign@cyber.net

Copyright® 1996 by Linda M. Ramsay
Edited by Mary Jo Mathews
First Printing 1996
Printed and bound in the United States of America
10 9 8 7 6 5 4 3 2 1

Publisher's Cataloging in Publication

Ramsay, Linda M., 1955—
Interior Design-Furnishings Directory of Discounted 800-Number and Hard-to-Find Companies: *Insider's Home Decorating Guide of Lower-Priced and Little-Known Sources that Offer You Substantial Savings and Higher Values*

p. cm.
Includes index
Preassigned LCCN: 94-090784
ISBN 0-9629918-2-1 $19.99

ATTENTION: ORGANIZATIONS, UNIVERSITIES, CORPORATIONS: This book is available at quantity discounts on bulk purchases for educational, business, or sales promotional use. For information, please contact our Sales Department, Touch of Design®, 475 College Blvd., Ste. 6290, Oceanside, CA 92057. (619) 945-7909, todesign@cybernet.

Table of Contents

Introduction

This is a comprehensive guide for purchasing interior furnishings at enormous savings from mail order and hard-to-find sources. You never need to pay premium prices (or so called sale prices) for interior products again. Buy direct or through a lower-priced distributor and cut your costs down enormously.

Most resalers price their products up two (if you really shop around) to four times the product's cost and then discount the price slightly and call it a "sale price." This catalog lists many companies and distributors that sell their goods and services "wholesale" at 30% to 90% below list or retail prices. Part of the reason for these lower prices are the regular retailers' high overhead. They must pay salaries, commissions, rent, advertising, insurance costs, storage costs, large utility bills, and other miscellaneous costs.

This directory has been developed for consumers, decorators and designers who wish to stretch their decorating dollars as far as they can. Design professionals are able to find new sources to buy interior products for their customers less expensively. Non-stocking Designers will find furniture sources that will sell to them. This guide will allow you to buy more while spending less and, therefore, get the most value for the money spent.

Interior designers and decorators will find that, in many cases, they can find new, otherwise unknown, sources to buy interior products from that outdo the prices and quality they are presently paying and providing. They will find many companies listed in this directory that offer products they would otherwise never have known about.

Buying by mail or phone is now very easy due to 800 numbers and credit cards. Mail-order and phone-order shopping are also timesaving and convenient.

Comparison shop via 800 numbers between companies on their shipping costs, return policies, sales tax (you do not usually pay sales tax, if you are out of their state), and product and company guarantees before placing an order. Interior design business owners when placing an order, ask for wholesale pricing.

The reasons you save more money by buying via a wholesaler or discounter are:

- They have lower overhead costs and are, therefore, able to pass the savings on to the consumer and offer lower wholesale pricing to resellers. They usually do not have as many salaries to pay, high rents or mortgages, and other related costs for running a retail store or other establishment.

- They have a lower profit margin. Discounters and wholesalers sell in much larger volume compared to retail operations. They make a larger quantity of sales compared to a department store or small shop, so they can afford to make less money on each sale.

- They generally do little advertising and, thus, have lower advertising costs. They generally run ads in magazines at remnant rates, and do not usually run ads constantly in newspapers or utilize direct mail (very expensive).

Companies are run by people. Naturally, some people are more efficient than others.

After a period of time, when contacting some of the companies below, you may find some of the companies have gone out of business, changed their name, changed their address, and/or changed what products they offer. Some companies change from directly selling their products to only selling wholesale to distributors. When contacted, these companies will usually supply literature about their products and their distributors' phone numbers and addresses.

Many times requests for catalogs and information go unanswered due to negligent and/or inadequate employees or the post office mishandling your requests for information. We have written to each company listed in this directory for correct information on products, their mailing addresses, phone numbers, etc. We have tried to be as accurate as possible. What is printed here is what has been supplied to us at the time of the publication date.

Most companies offer catalogs, literature or product brochures showing their line of products. Firms constantly revise and change their catalogs and literature. After an information request, if you don't receive a response from the company after 10 days, call or write to the company again and request their literature once again. For literature requests, many firms ask for an SASE (a #10 size, self-addressed, stamped envelope). If you ignore their request for an SASE, don't expect a response from the company. This is their way of cutting their costs down in providing customers with literature.

Some of the companies listed do not have a telephone number listed. They are set up to only work with you by mail order. Several companies have only phone numbers listed, they want to be phoned for information.

When you are ready to place your order from information provided by a company, be sure the pricing information is current. Prices do change without notice as do available products. Call or write and ask for a current price list. If you don't, expect to be charged the difference between the old price and the new price after you receive the ordered item.

Some companies do *not* have catalogs or literature for distribution. They operate with a price-quote type of system. You find the desired item's manufacturer's name and model number (SKU number) and call or write the company for a price quote. A price quote is the cost of that item from a particular firm. The firm will guarantee that price for a limited time only or until they run out of stock of that item.

Some companies, when making a price quote, will lump the shipping, handling, insurance, and sales tax (if applicable) all together in a lump final price quote. Make sure that each charge is broken down and itemized for you. This is important should you have to return the item later for a refund. If you don't have each charge itemized, you will be placed in a vulnerable position by the firm on the amounts you will or won't be refunded for these costs. Never expect to receive a refund on shipping and handling charges on mail-ordered items. This is a standard in the mail-order industry.

Most firms will prefer to give you price quotes over the phone. This saves them time and money mailing or FAXing you a hard copy of the quote. They can also cover themselves on misquoted prices this way. After all, you misunderstood.

Phone quotes are an easy way for you to save time and energy by calling around and getting instant prices. When calling for phone quotes, make sure you have all of the applicable information required right in front of you. Remember, the *most important price* is the delivered price of the product.

Should you get a favorable price or desire to buy from a particular firm, have them mail you a detailed quote. This gives you a record of the quoted price, the name of the person who gave you the quote, and all the details about the item and its extra options recorded in writing. Review the quote and make sure the price quoter clearly understood *what* they were asked for a price on.

When requesting a quote by letter, include all pertinent information about the desired item. List an area in the letter with blanks next to them to break down the itemized charges as shown. Again, this is your insurance later, should you have to return the item and expect to recover most of your money.

Price   _____
Insurance   _____
Shipping/Handling   _____
Other Charges   _____
Sales Tax   _____
Total Price   _____

Inquire in your letter to the quoting company, as to how long they will honor the quoted price. Never ask for more than three quotes at one time or you will probably not get a quote at all. If you include an SASE, you make it easier and quicker for the firm to repond back to you, so do it.

Disclaimer

This directory is designed to provide information about the subject matters covered. Great care has been taken to ensure the accuracy and utility of the information included within this book. It is sold with the understanding that the publisher and the author are not engaged in rendering any type of professional advice or in recommending or referring you to any particular companies. Information provided has been provided by the companies listed. If legal advice or other expert professional advice is required, the services of a competent professional person should be sought. Every effort has been made to make this book as complete as possible.

Neither Touch of Design®, nor the author, Linda Ramsay, assume any responsibility or liability for errors, inaccuracies, omissions, use, application of information, selection of any company or distributor, selection of products, or any other inconsistency herein. The author and Touch of Design® shall have neither liability nor responsibility to any person or entity with respect to any loss or damage caused, or alleged to be caused, directly or indirectly, by the information contained in this book.

Therefore, this text should be used only as a general guide and not as the ultimate source on interior-design information or suppliers. Furthermore, this book contains information on interior-design furnishings current with the printing date. The purpose of this book is to educate on what alternate sources are available for purchasing interior-design furnishings. Any slight against any organizations or manufacturers is unintentional.

In the following listings, the claims noted are not Touch of Design's® opinions. Most times, the affirmations are the claims of the company listed. Compare prices, warranties, shipping costs, etc., over the phone and in writing when getting quotes.

Purchasing Guidelines

Services Provided by Purchasing Through a Decorator or a Retailer

Before making a decision that you will buy your design products direct from a manufacturer or distributor, consider the following services you receive by buying retail.

A decorator or retailer will:

- Provide product knowledge. They will be able to advise you on whether the treatment or product you are considering for purchase will function as you expect it to.

- Make suggestions regarding the advantages and disadvantages of different products and treatments.

- Have design training and experience.

- Help you make the right decisions on which product to buy for your needs and requirements.

- Have fiber and fabric knowledge.

- Have knowledge of construction quality.

- Usually measure and take responsibility for the correctness of the measurements, if you have their company install the products.

- Calculate the correct amount of yardage required for the job, taking into account fabric, wallcovering, and floorcovering-design repeats. They will usually not sell you an insufficient or an excessive amount of yardage to complete the job.

- Provide tips for installing their products for do-it-yourselfers.

- Will assist you in problem solving.

- Take care of shipping and product-defect problems and provide for the return of the product if the need should arise.

- Provide brand name or pattern advice.

- Coordinate professional installation or refer installers to you to do the job. Due to construction deficiencies, many times, installers have to make adjustments during the course of the installation to make products fit correctly.

General Guidelines for Maximizing
Benefits and Limiting Risks

When buying direct from a manufacturer or distributor, consider the following:

- Most distributors take Visa and Mastercards. Others also take American Express and Discover cards. Some allow C.O.D. orders. Because of the acceptance of these credit methods, ordering is easy.

- Merchant accounts (seller accounts for Visa, Mastercard, American Express, Discover, etc.) are hard to get and many times expensive to set up for many companies. They are also hard to keep. Merchants are allowed only a few charge backs (disputed charges by customers) before a merchant account may be terminated. Once a company loses its merchant account, they have to immediately reapply, pay more application fees, and repeat the credit approval process of re-obtaining another account. Therefore, when purchasing with credit cards, you have more leverage with the seller to correct problems than if you pay by other methods.

- Most companies automatically give you a satisfaction guarantee (even if *not* noted in their directory listing). Ask them. If you pay by Visa, Mastercard, Discover card, etc., again, you do have recourse through these processors should you not be satisfied with the purchased products or services. In case of a problem, credit-card processors will help you get a refund. Review the **important** point below.

- Generally, you are not charged sales tax if you reside outside of the state of the listed company or distributor. This may change in the future, since most states *want* sales-tax revenue. For listings in states other than your own, inquire if you must pay sales tax.

- Most products are for immediate delivery. **Exceptions:** special-ordered furniture, custom-made window treatments, and other custom-made items.

- Most wallpaper distributors offer free shipping. Ask if the shipping is free. If you don't make an inquiry, expect to be charged.

- Most distributors offer first-quality goods. Inquire about the level of quality before making a final decision on *who* to buy from.

- Although two like products may *appear* the same, products are definitely different quality from brand to brand and from model to model. Compare all materials, finishes, and construction.

- Not every item carried by a company will be listed in this directory. If a compatible product is listed, chances are the listed company may also carry similar or related products. Call or write to the company and ask for their catalog or brochure on their offered products.

- Many discounters charge for their catalogs. They do not want to pay shipping costs, printing costs, and other costs of materials for customers that indiscriminately request them as idea books. Charging for materials is their way of prequalifying a customer. They realize only serious customers will pay the catalog charge.

  Charges for catalogs and information are usually "refundable" against the first order. Many times a coupon will be enclosed with the catalog to use as a refund when you place an order or you will be asked to simply deduct the price of the catalog from your total price at the time you place your order. If you don't place an order, you don't get a refund. After you establish yourself as a buyer, you will tend to get periodic mailings and regular catalogs from the discounter.

  For literature or catalogues costing up to $1, just enclose a dollar or sandwich coins between two pieces of cardboard. Enclose a check or money orders for literature over a dollar. Do not use stamps or credit cards to pay for nominal catalog charges, unless you are specifically requested to do so.

- Catalog showrooms are another alternative discount-buying source. Depending on your locale, you may or may not have access to one. They may or may not charge an annual fee for belonging to the "club" and generally will work with you in this manner: you find what you want elsewhere and bring in the measurements, manufacturer's name, stock, model, or item number, pattern name or code, and color name and number. This information can be found on tags on products in stores or in manufacturer's literature and catalogs. When using manufacturer's literature for this information, use the manufacturer's information and numbers and not the retailer's ordering information. Many retailers "private label" or use their own labeling system for their goods to make it difficult for you to obtain manufacturer information, names, and numbers. This makes it harder for customers to shop their prices or buy it elsewhere for less.

  Buying clubs will look up the item in their extensive supply of wholesaler and distributor catalogues and see if they can get the item for you. If they can, the price is usually a good one. They will penalize you if they have to take the item back, as they won't be able to resell it to someone else, and there will be costs incurred in the shipping back and forth and restocking charges with the manufacturer. In the case of custom goods, you designed the item and, therefore, it is not returnable.

- Other types of firms that use price-quote systems operate as the catalog showrooms do in the above catalog showroom listing. Do the legwork first and find out what you want price quotes on *exactly* before you start calling around or writing to the manufacturers and using their time. Specify brand, style, and color for quotes.

- Compare the prices quotes from discounters out of your locale against prices you can get locally. Include any shipping costs in your total prices. Determine if you pay sales tax and add this cost into the total price. Although you probably will save on sales tax (if purchased from another state than the one you reside in), you will get the product serviced easier and less expensively (you usually won't pay shipping costs to send the item back) if bought locally. Take into consideration other local shopping costs, such as mileage, time, and parking fees.

- Most companies offer the full manufacturer's warranty. Inquire when you call for price quotes. Also inquire what their return policy is, should you be dissatisfied.

- Most companies will ship anywhere in the U.S.A. and some to Canada. Ask.

- Get the name of the person with whom you are dealing over the telephone. By asking for names, you automatically put the salesperson on the alert to provide you with better service. You will also have a person to refer back to, should a problem arise.

- Should you have doubts about the company, product quality, service, etc., order only one item to "test" the company before placing a larger order. See what quality product is provided and how the company performs.

- If you have doubts about a company's reputation or level of service, check with the Better Business Bureau in the company's community for registered complaints and/or membership.

- Ask for and call referrals of satisfied customers.

- Note any minimum-order requirements. Do you meet the requirements? If not, call and ask if the requirement is mandatory. Many times, companies are more flexible than they appear in writing.

- Read our books, *Secrets of Success for Today's Interior Designers and Decorators* or *Successful Window Dressing and Interior Design* (ordering information in the back of this book), to find out which product or products to select for your situation, how to measure each product, what the requirements are for each product, what is standard, and what are available as options. These books will take you by the hand and turn you into a fabric and window-treatment expert.

Important Note: Whenever returning *anything*, pay for a post-office receipt of mailing or a return receipt. If you do not get a receipt, it is your word against the merchant's that you returned the item. Even the credit-card companies will not stand behind you, should a dispute arise between you and the seller. A receipt is your proof that you *did* return the item.

Measuring and Installation
of Window Treatments

If you do not feel confident in your window-measuring skills even after reading *Secrets of Success for Today's Interior Designers and Decorators* or *Successful Window Dressing and Interior Design*, then you will need to find an installer to measure for the window treatments for you. You can easily find a competent window-treatment installer by doing one of the following:

- Check your telephone book's yellow pages under drapery installation or window-blind installation headings.

- Call and ask your local department store window-treatment ready-made department for a recommendation.

- Call and ask your local department store custom-decorating desk for a recommendation. Many of their installers do side jobs after hours and on weekends.

- Get estimates from a decorator for the desired window treatments. Ask the estimating decorator if their installer also works independently for customers. Tell the decorator that you have several blinds or drapery rods that need to be installed for other windows. Purchase one or two simple window treatments from the decorator. Ask the installer when he or she comes out if they will work for you. Have the installer measure and write down the required sizes while they are in your home on their first trip. This will save them time and an extra trip charge for you. Pay them or lavishly tip them for this extra service. Get their home phone number and contact them when the window treatments arrive.

Important Note: When giving sizes and measurements for window coverings, width measurements are *always* stated first, then followed by the length measurement. Window-treatment selection and measuring are both complicated and must be very precise. I cannot emphasize enoough the importance of reviewing one of the two books noted above to alleviate many, many measuring and buying errors. At the very *least*, review all literature and other materials provided by the companies you contact about their products.

Placing an Order

When you are ready to place a phone order with a company, follow this procedure. Should you place your order in writing by mail or FAX, adapt the following accordingly. Make sure to make a copy of the order for your record and file it with the corresponding company catalog or literature.

1. Have the catalog or corresponding ordering literature in front of you. Tell the salesperson about any coupons or refunds for the purchase of literature due you at the time of the inital order.

2. Have your credit card out and ready. Make sure you have enough credit open to buy to cover the item and that the credit card has not expired.

3. Decide where you want to have the item delivered. Have ready the complete address, ZIP code, and an alternate phone number.

4. To avoid mistakes, prefill out the order form so all pertinent information is decided and recorded. If you don't have an order form, note manufacturer name, SKU, stock, model numbers, or item number, pattern name or code, color name and number, sizes, and measurements.

5. Ask and note the name of the person taking the order. Also, note the time and day.

6. Inquire if the item is stocked or has to be special ordered.

7. Ask when the order will ship and arrive approximately.

8. Inquire if all items will ship together.

9. Ask for a total price, including sales tax and shipping. If it varies from what you have been previously quoted, ask for an explanation.

10. Make an inquiry as to what the company's return policy is and what the warranties are for the specific item, if you don't already have them in writing.

Source Directory

Interior Design Computer Bulletin Board

Touch of Design ®
475 College Blvd., Ste. 6290
Oceanside, CA 92057
(619) 945-4283 bulletin board
accessable via computer modem
(619) 945-7909 voice
We are setting up a bulletin board
(BBS) for designers, decorators and
consumers of interior design to
address problems, concerns,
resources, etc. Everyone who calls
can access the questions and the
answers and participate. We will have
our interior-design book catalog and
reports will be online and available to
download, free. Our internet email
address is: todesign@cyber.net.

Miniblinds, Wood Blinds, Vertical Blinds, Pleated Shades, Duette Shades, and Window Shades

3-Day Blinds
Mail Order Dept.
2220 E. Cuneate Ave.
Anaheim, CA 92806
(800) 966-NOID
Free information and ordering kit.
Savings on all types of miniblinds,
vertical blinds, wood blinds, and
pleated shades. Lifetime guarantee.

$5 Wallcovering Co.
374 Hall St.
Phoenixville, PA 19460
(800) 5-Dollar
Call for information. Discounted
prices on wallcoverings. Up to 80
percent savings on custom blinds.

Advanced Consumer Products
P.O. Box 95
Garden City, MI 48135-0095
(800) 677-9090
Free information. Up to 80 percent
savings on miniblinds and 75 percent
on vertical blinds. Save also on pleated

shades, Duettes and wood blinds.
Most major brands are available and
discounted. Blinds ship within 5 days
or they are free!

All-States Decorating Network
1605 Badger, Ste. 206
Toms River, NJ 08755
(800) 334-8590
Free information. Savings up to 82
percent on all types of first-quality
miniblinds, vertical blinds, wood blinds,
pleated shades, and toppers. Lifetime
guarantee. Will beat anyone's prices
right down to their cost price. Free
UPS shipping. Business established 20
years ago.

American Blind & Wallpaper Factory
28237 Orchard Lake Rd.
Farmington Hills, MI 48334
(800) 735-5300
Call for free information and blind
sample kit. Up to 78 percent savings
on wallcoverings, up to 80 percent on

mini and micro blinds, 75 percent on wood blinds, vertical blinds, custom-made roller shades, and pleated shades. Free UPS shipping.

American Discount Wallcoverings
1411 5th Ave.
Pittsburgh, PA 15219
(800) 777-2737
Free brochure. Save from 15 to 50 percent on wallpaper, window treatments, and upholstery fabrics.

Around the Window
326 N. Stonestreet Ave., Ste. 204
Rockville, MD 20850
(800) 642-9899
Call for designer sample kit. Up to 76 percent savings on national brands of miniblinds, vertical blinds, pleated shades, specialty-shaped blinds and shades. Lifetime guarantee.

BLINDBUSTERS
10858 Harry Hines Blvd.
Dallas TX 75220
(800) 883-5000
Free information. They sell complete packages of blinds starting at $299.00 (miniblinds, vertical blinds and pleated shades — can be mixed and matched). Savings on wood blinds, Duettes, verticals, and pleated shades (with or without privacy backing).

Blind Center USA, Inc.
30242 Littlecroft
Houston, TX 77386
(800) 676-5029
Free information. Up to 81 percent savings on wood blinds, miniblinds, all types of pleated shades, and Duettes. Free shipping.

Blind Works
1605 Badger Dr.
Toms River, NJ 08755
(800) 334-8590

Free information. First-quality goods. All major brands and types of window coverings. Up to 80 percent savings off department store prices on miniblinds, vertical blinds and Duettes. Decorator fabrics are available. Free UPS shipping.

Blinds 'N Things
516 Jefferson Blvd.
Birmingham, AL 35217
(800) 662-5894
(800) 824-0632 AL residents
Free information. Save from 50 to 60 percent on micro and miniblinds.

Blinds Today
P.O. Box 218
Normal, IL 61761
(800) 336-1611
Call for free information. Up to 75 percent savings on blinds and shades.

Bradd & Hall Blinds
7234 New Market Ct.
Manassas, VA 22110
(800) 542-7502
Free information. Up to 80 percent savings on blinds.

Brentwood Manor Furnishings
316 Virginia Ave.
Clarksville, VA 23927
(800) 225-6105
Free brochure on fine-quality, name-brand furniture. Factory-direct prices on hundreds of brands of furniture, window treatments, draperies, accessories, clocks, and mirrors.

Bryne Home Furnishings
3516 W. Magnolia Blvd.
Burbank, CA 91505
(800) 660-3516
Call for information and quotes. 25 to 40 percent savings on furniture,

carpeting, draperies, and mattresses. Authorized dealer for Hickory, Century, Waterford, and 100 other quality lines.

Calico Corners
203 Gale Ln.
Kennett Square, PA 19348
(800) 777-9933
Call for the store nearest you. Save 30 to 60 percent on interior fabrics. Decorative fabric chain that sells fabrics at reduced prices. Vast selection of in-stock fabrics. They also fabricate custom drapery, bedspreads, and fabric accessories.

Colorel Blinds
8200 E. Park Meadows Dr.
Littleton, CO 80124
(800) 877-4800
Free information. Up to 81 percent savings on blinds and other window coverings. One-day delivery.

The Decorator's Edge, Inc.
509 Randolph St.
Thomasville, NC 27360
(800) 289-5589
(910) 476-1047
Custom window treatments and interiors. Save up to 75% off retail on mini and micro blinds, 70% off on wood blinds, 60% off on vertical blinds, 20 to 40% off on fabrics, 20 to 40% off on wallpaper, 20 to 50% off on furniture.

Devenco Products, Inc.
Box 700
Decatur, GA 30031
(404) 378-4597
Free information on period reproductions of wood blinds and shutters.

Direct Wallpaper Express
374 Hall St.
Phoenixville, PA 19460
(800) 336-9255
Save 40 to 72 percent on name brands of wallpaper and window treatments. Pattern identification service.

Express Blinds Factory
326 N. Stonestreet Ave., Ste. 204
Rockville, MD 20850
(800) 642-9899
Free designer sample kit and information. Up to 76 percent savings on miniblinds, vertical blinds, and pleated shades. Their line of products includes most major brands and they do specialty windows (skylights, arches, octagon, and inclines). Lifetime guarantee. 24-hour shipping is available.

Fabric Shop
120 N. Seneca Ave.
Shippensburg, PA 17257
(800) 233-7012
Send SASE for free information. Decorator, drapery, and upholstery fabrics. Custom made drapery, top treatments, bedspreads, and accessories.

Fabrics by Phone
P.O. Box 309
Walnut Bottom, PA 17266
(800) 233-7012
$3 for brochure of a line of decorator and drapery fabrics. Custom-made drapery, top treatments, bedspreads, accessories.

Factory Paint Store
505 Pond St.
South Weymouth, MA 02190
(617) 331-1200
Free information. Their line of products include window shades, wallpaper, paint and lighting fixtures.

Headquarters Windows & Walls
8 Clinton Pl.
Morristown, NJ 07960
(800) 338-4882
Free information. Up to 80 percent savings on micro, mini, Duettes, wood blinds, verticals, pleated shades, and toppers. Up to 81 percent savings on wallpaper. Free shipping.

Home Fashion Center
R.R.2, Box 344A
Columbia, MO 65201-9802
Discounts up to 50 percent on wall-coverings, window blinds, carpet, and floorcoverings.

MDC Direct, Inc.
P.O. 569
Marietta, GA 30061
(800) 892-2083
Free information and samples. Up to 82 percent savings on all types of miniblinds, wood blinds, pleated shades, vertical blinds, and Duettes. They also manufacture bedspreads and draperies. Free UPS shipping.

Mr. Miniblind
Call the 800 directory for the nearest store near you. Discounted prices on miniblinds, vertical blinds, pleated shades, and Duettes. Fast delivery.

Nation Wide Wholesalers
P.O. Box 40
Hackensack, NJ 07602
(800) 488-WALL
Free information and vertical blind kit. Up to 78 percent savings on wallcoverings, 80 percent on all types of blinds, and up to 60 percent on decorator fabrics. Savings also on wallcoverings. First-quality goods. NJ an NY residents pay sales tax. Free UPS delivery.

National Blind and Wallpaper Factory
400 Galleria, #400
Southfield, MI 48034
(800) 477-8000
They've merged with Style Wallcovering and Mary's Wallpaper to become the largest mail-order dis-counter, bringing you unbeatable buying power! Up to 80 percent off all name brands with free shipping within 48 hours! Free blind sample kit.

The Paper Place Interiors
606 Idol Dr.
P.O. Box 5985
High Point, NC 27262
(910) 869-8752
$3 for information. Discount prices on 200 lines of name-brand wallcoverings, fabrics, blinds, shades, and woven woods. Including Del Mar window coverings, Dapha furniture, Marbro lamps, and Masland carpet.

Post Wallcovering Distributors
2065 Franklin
Bloomfield Hills, MI 48013
(800) 521-0650
Free information. Up to 75 percent savings on blinds. Up to 70 percent savings on wallpaper.

Premier Blind Co.
317 E. Hempstead
Giddings, TX 78942
(800) 441-1288
Free information and color samples. Up to 80 percent savings on mini and micro blinds, verticals, pleated shades, Duettes, and custom drapery. Free UPS shipping.

Quix 1
P.O. Box 5659
Pittsburgh PA 15207
(800) 487-6773
Up to 60 percent savings on fabrics

from almost any mill or distributor. Over 500 companies represented. Wholesale prices on miniblinds, vertical blinds, and shades.

Qwik Blinds
1925 S. Vineyard Ave.
Ontario, CA 91761
(800) 325-4637
Free order and sample kit. Save 50 to 91 percent on miniblinds, woods, verticals, and cellular shades. 100 percent satisfaction guaranteed.

Shaker Workshops
P.O. Box 1028-CL14
Concord, MA 01742
(617) 646-8985
$1 for 56-page catalog. Collection of Shaker rockers, dining chairs, tables, beds, miscellaneous furniture, and an assortment of Shaker accessories. Available in kits or custom finished.

Silver's Wholesale Club
3001-15 Kensington Ave.
Philadelphia, PA 19134
(800) 426-6600
Free information. Up to 81 percent savings on first-quality wallcoverings, blinds, and verticals. Free delivery.

Spiegel Catalog
P.O. Box 6340
Chicago, IL 60680-6340
(800) 345-4500
$3 charge for catalog. Full range of interior products, furniture, curtains, draperies, accessories, rugs, lamps, etc. Many items discounted or available discounted through subsequent sale catalogs. Satisfaction guaranteed.

U.S.A. Blind Factory
1312 Live Oak
Houston, TX 77003
(800) 275-3219

Free information and sample kit. Up to 80 percent savings on mini and micro blinds, vertical blinds, wood blinds, and pleated shades.

Wallpaperxpress
P.O. Box 4061
Naperville, IL 60567
(800) 288-9979
Free information. Up to 70 percent savings on wallpaper, 25 percent savings on decorator fabrics, 60 percent savings on blinds.

WE R Fabrics
963 Lomas Sante Fe Dr.
Solana Beach, CA (619) 755-1175
or
Mission Viejo CA (714) 770-4662
Check your yellow pages for other locations near you. Discounted source for decorator and upholstery fabrics. Custom-made drapery, valances, bedspreads and fabric accessories, upholstery and slipcovers.

Wells Interiors
7171 Amador Valley Plaza Rd.
Dublin, CA 94568
(800) 547-8982
Free catalog and window covering kits. They offer a guarantee to beat other dealer's prices on miniblinds, wood blinds, vertical blinds, pleated shades, Duettes, and woven woods.

The Wholesale Blind Co.
P.O. Box 2005
Laurel, MS 39442
(800) 523-6276
Free information. Discounted prices on various types of miniblinds, 1" & 2" wide wood blinds, vertical blinds, and softlight shades.

Wholesale Verticals, Inc.
P.O. Box 305
Baldwin, NY 11510

(800) 762-2748
Free designer kit. Up to 80 percent savings on miniblinds and verticals. Also savings on Graber drapery hardware. Free UPS shipping.

Window Scapes
11211 Sorrento Valley Rd.
San Diego, CA 92121
(800) 786-3021
Up to 80 percent savings on vertical blinds, pleated shades, wood blinds and various types of miniblinds.

Window Express
32525 Stephenson Hwy.
Madison Heights, MI 48071
(800) 772-1947, (800) 777-7747
Discounted prices on miniblinds and verticals. Super savings on wallpaper. Free shipping for most items.

**Worldwide Wallcoverings
and Blinds, Inc.**
333 Skokie Blvd.
Northbrook, IL 60062
(800) 322-5400
Free ordering kit for blinds. Up to 80 percent savings on miniblinds, vertical blinds, Duettes, and pleated shades. Up to 78 percent savings on wall-coverings. Special wallpaper case discounts. Free U.P.S. shipping within 3 days.

Yankee Wallcoverings, Inc.
109 Accord Park Dr.
Norwell, MA 02061
(800) 624-7711
Free information. Savings from 35-75 percent on coordinating wallcoverings and fabrics.

Yield House
P.O. Box 5000
North Conway, NH 03860
(800) 258-4720
Free information. They offer

country curtains, accessories, collectibles, and furniture.

Yorktowne Wallpaper Outlet
2445 S. Queen St.
York, PA 17402
(800) 847-6142
Free information. 30 to 70 percent savings on wallcoverings.

Curtains and Fabric Panels

Arizona Mail Order
(800) 362-8415
$2 for Home Etc. catalog featuring discounted prices on all types of bedding and bath ensembles, bedspreads, quilts, linens, accessories, curtains, and rugs.

Laura Ashley
1300 MacArthur Blvd.
Mahwah, NJ 07430
(800) 223-6917
$4 for catalog featuring English period reproductions of window treatments, fabrics, bedspreads, and other accessories.

At Home in the Valley
P.O. Box 7303
Van Nuys, CA 91409
(818) 780-4663
$1 for catalog of braided rugs, chair pads, placemats, and curtains.

Constance Carol
P.O. Box 899
Plymouth, MA 02360
(800) 343-5921
Free catalog of stencil designs and curtains. Charge for swatches.

Caroline Country Ruffles
420 W. Frandkin Blvd.
Gastonia, NC 28052
(800) 426-1039
$2 for catalog of curtains, jabots, cascades, swags, blouson valances, balloon curtains, bedspreads, comforters, and fabric accessories. Range of fabrics. Satisfaction guaranteed.

Colonial Country Originals, Inc.
P.O. Box 2010
Hanover, MA 02339
(800) 627-2878

$3 for catalog of reproduction Colonial and Early-American curtains in a range of fabrics.

Connecticut Curtain Company
Commerce Plaza, Rt. 6
Danbury, CT 06810
(800) 732-4549, (203) 798-1850
$2 for catalog. 20 to 40 percent savings on window treatment hardware. Iron and steel curtain rods, wooden rods, hard-to-fit corner, arched or palladian rods, holdbacks, swagholders, and basic rods.

Laura Copenhaver Industries, Inc.
P.O. Box 149
Marion, VA 24354
(800) 227-6797
Free color brochure of handmade canopies, coverlets, dust ruffles, and curtains. In-stock items or custommade. Satisfaction guaranteed. Business established in 1916.

Country Curtains
Red Lion Inn
Stockbridge, MA 01262
Free 72-page catalog of countrystyled curtains in cottons and cotton blends, bedding, lamps, and accessories.

Designer Secrets
Box 529
Fremont, NE 68025
$2 for catalog. Up to 50 percent savings on window treatments, wallpaper, accessories, fabrics, bedspreads, and some furniture.

Dianthus, LTD
P.O. Box 870
Plymouth, MA 02362
(508) 747-4179
$4 for catalog of country-classic

curtains and accessories.

Domestications
P.O. Box 40
Hanover, PA 17333-0040
(800) 746-2555
Free catalog of discounted bedroom
ensembles, curtains, accessories, and
lamps.

Dorothy's Ruffled Originals
6721 Market St.
Wilmington, NC 28405
$4 for catalog of ruffled curtains and
fabric accessories. Range of fabrics.

Especially Lace
202 5th St.
West Des Moines, IA 50265
(515) 277-8778
$3.50 for catalog of lace European
curtains and valances.

Fabrics by Phone
P.O. Box 309
Walnut Bottom, PA 17266
(800) 233-7012
(800) 692-7345 PA res.
$3 for information and fabric samples
of custom-made drapery and fabric
accessories.

Fabric Shop
120 N. Seneca Ave.
Shippensburg, PA 17257
(800) 233-7012
(800) 692-7345 PA residents
Send SASE for information on
custom-made drapery and fabric
accessories, featuring a range of
drapery and upholstery fabrics.

Faith's Lacery
89 W. Main St.
Dundee, IL 60118
$2 for catalog offering all types of lace
window treatments and accessories.

The Gazebo of New York
127 East 57th St., Dept. CL
New York, NY 10022
$6 for catalog of a large selection
of quilts, duvet covers, dust ruffles,
curtains, braided and rag rugs, pillows,
antique and new wicker pieces, and
other hand-crafted accessories.

Virginia Goodwin
Rt. 2, Box 770
Boone, NC 28607
(800) 735-5191
$1 for information on their line of
drapery, valances, canopies, bedspreads, and dust ruffles.

Linen & Lace
#4 Lafayette
Washington, MO 63090
(800) 332-LACE
$2 for catalog of imported Scottish
lace curtains, Victorian gifts and accessories.

The Linen Source
5401 Hangar Court
Tampa, FL 33631-3151
(800) 431-2620
Free catalog of discounted
bedroom ensembles, curtains, accessories, and rugs. Satisfaction
guaranteed.

London Lace
167 Newbury St.
Boston, MA 02116
(617) 267-3506
$2 for catalog of lace window
treatments.

Mather's Department Store
31 E. Main St.
Westminster, MD 21157
(410) 848-6410
Free catalog of country-styled curtains
and valances in a range of fabrics.

Montgomery Ward Direct
(800) 852-2711
Call for a free catalog featuring discounted prices on bedding and bath ensembles, bedspreads, accessories, curtains, rugs, bedroom, living and family room furniture.

The Renovator's Supply
Renovator's Old Mill
Millers Falls, MA 01349
(413) 659-2211
$3 for catalog of reproduction curtains, accessories, antique hardware, lighting, rugs, bathroom and plumbing fixtures.

Rue DE France
78 Thames St.
Newport, RI 02840
(800) 777-0998
$3 for catalog of their line of lace curtains and accessories.

Seraph
5606 State Rt. 37
Delaware, OH 43015
(614) 369-1817
They offer a collection of coordinated window treatments, bedroom ensembles, rugs, and accessories.

Spiegel Catalog
P.O. Box 6340
Chicago, IL 60680-6340
(800) 345-4500
$3 for catalog. Full range of interior products, furniture, curtains, draperies, accessories, rugs, lamps, etc. Many items discounted or available discounted through subsequent sale catalogs. Satisfaction guaranteed.

Touch of Class
Order Dept.
1905 N. Van Buren St.
Huntingburg, IN 47542
(800) 457-7456

Free catalog of bedroom and bathroom ensembles. Bedspreads, curtains, drapery, fabric accessories, bathroom accessories, lamps, and miscellaneous related accessories.

Vintage Valances
P.O. Box 43326
Cincinnati, OH 45243
(513) 561-8665
$10 for catalog and fabric samples. Victorian- and Greek-styled valances.

Quilts and Bedding

American Quilter's Society
P.O. Box 3290
Paducah, KY 42002-3290
$5 for color catalog of over one
hundred and thirty quilts for sale from
the members of the American Quilter's Society. 15-day money-back
guarantee on quilt purchases.

The Antique Quilt Source
385 Springview Rd.
Carlisle, PA 17013
(717) 245-2054
$6 for current catalog and photos.
Unique selection of antique quilts
from Pennsylvania. Excellent con-
dition. Satisfaction guaranteed.

Arizona Mail Order
(800) 362-8415
$2 for Home Etc. catalog featuring
discounted prices on all types of bedding and bath ensembles, bedspreads,
quilts, linens, accessories, curtains,
rugs, bedroom, living and family room
furniture.

Laura Ashley
1300 MacArthur Blvd.
Mahwah NJ 07430
(800) 223-6917
$4 for catalog of English period
reproductions of window treatments,
fabrics, bedspreads, and other
accessories.

Caroline Country Ruffles
420 W. Frandkin Blvd.
Gastonia, NC 28052
(800) 426-1039
$2 for catalog of curtains, jabots,
cascades, swags, blouson valances,
balloon curtains, bedspreads,
comforters, and fabric accessories.
Range of fabrics. Satisfaction
guaranteed.

Cindy's Corner
109 Freeman's Bridge Rd.
Scotia, NY 12302
(518) 377-6576
$5 for catalog and swatches featuring
reasonably-priced, quality quilts and
accessories.

Country Curtains
Red Lion Inn
Stockbridge, MA 01262
Free 72-page catalog of country-
styled curtains in cottons and cotton
blends, bedding, lamps, and accessories.

Designer Secrets
Box 529
Fremont, NE 68025
$2 for catalog. Up to 50 percent
savings on window treatments, wallpaper, accessories, fabrics, bedspreads,
and some furniture.

Domestications
P.O. Box 40
Hanover, PA 17333-0040
(800) 746-2555
Free catalog of discounted bedroom
ensembles, curtains, accessories, and
lamps.

Down Home Factory Outlet
85 Rte. 46 West
Towawa, NJ 07512
(800) ALL-Down
Free catalog offering down comforters,
pillows, and other bedding supplies at
wholesale prices.

Down-Time
P.O. Box 296
Wabash, IN 46992
(800) 638-3696
Goose-down comforters at wholesale
prices. Satisfaction guaranteed.

The Gazebo of New York
127 East 57th St., Dept. CL
New York, NY 10022
$6 for catalog of a large selection
of quilts, duvet covers, dust ruffles,
curtains, braided and rag rugs, pillows,
antique and new wicker pieces, and
other hand-crafted accessories.

Virginia Goodwin
Rt. 2, Box 770
Boone, NC 28607
(800) 735-5191
$1 for information on their line of
drapery, valances, canopies, bedspreads, and dust ruffles.

Harris Levy, Inc.
278 Grand St.
New York, NY 10002
(800) 221-7750
(212) 226-3102 NY residents
Free information and savings of up to
40 percent off retail on bed, table, and
bath linens from all over the world.

Madison Quilt Shop
2307 Grand Concourse
Bronx, NY 10468
Send for information on their line of
quilts and other fabric accessories.

Montgomery Ward Direct
(800) 852-2711
Call for a free catalog featuring
discounted prices on all types of
bedding and bath ensembles, bedspreads, accessories, curtains, rugs,
bedroom, living and family room
furniture.

Muckleberry Farms
1240 Lynway Lane
Atlanta, GA 30311
$3 for catalog of their collection of
country quilts, wreaths, and accessories.

Olde Mill House Shoppe
105 Strasburg Pike
Lancaster, PA 17602
(717) 299-0678
$1 for catalog offering country-styled
furniture, bathroom accessories, linens,
braided rugs.

**Quality Furniture Market
of Lenoir, Inc.**
2034 Hickory Blvd., S.W.
Lenoir, NC 28645
Write for information. Discounts on
furniture, bedding, linens, accessories,
and lamp shades.

Quiltery
2030 Whitehall Ave.
Allentown, PA 18104
$2 for brochure of available quilts.

Rocky Mountain Quilts
2 Ocean Ave
Rockport, MA 01966
(800) 456-0892, (303) 464-7294
Quilts made from vintage fabrics,
antique and custom quilts, and quilt
restoration.

Touch of Class
Order Dept.
1905 N. Van Buren St.
Huntingburg, IN 47542
(800) 457-7456
Free catalog of bedroom and
bathroom ensembles. Bedspreads,
curtains, drapery, fabric accessories,
bathroom accessories, lamps, and
miscellaneous related accessories.

**Thomas K. Woodard
American Antiques & Quilts**
835 Madison Ave.
New York, NY 10021
(212) 988-2906
$5 for catalog of Early-American area
rugs and runners.

Drapery, Valances, Hardware, Bedspreads, Canopies, Linens and Fabric Accessories

All-States Decorating Network
1605 Badger, Ste. 206
Toms River, NJ 08755
(800) 334-8590
Free information. Up to 82 percent savings on all types of miniblinds, vertical blinds, wood blinds, pleated shades, and toppers. Lifetime guarantee. Will beat anyone's prices down to their cost. Free UPS shipping. Business established 20 years ago.

Arizona Mail Order
(800) 362-8415
$2 for Home Etc. catalog featuring discounted prices on all types of bedding and bath ensembles, bedspreads, quilts, linens, accessories, curtains, and rugs.

Laura Ashley
1300 MacArthur Blvd.
Mahwah NJ 07430
(800) 223-6917
$4 for catalog of English period reproductions of window treatments, fabrics, bedspreads, and other accessories.

At Home in the Valley
P.O. Box 7303
Van Nuys, CA 91409
(818) 780-4663
$1 for catalog of braided rugs, chair pads, placemats, and curtains.

The Atrium
430 S. Main St.
High Point, NC 27260
(910) 882-5599
Furniture mall of 35 discount galleries that represent over 650 furniture manufacturers. Offering all types of furnishings, including: accessories, Oriental rugs, lamps and lighting. Call to be directed to the gallery that carries specific lines of furnishings. Featuring nationwide delivery.

Brentwood Manor Furnishings
316 Virginia Ave.
Clarksville, VA 23927
(800) 225-6105
Free brochure on fine-quality, name-brand furniture. Factory-direct prices on hundreds of brands of furniture, window treatments, draperies, accessories and clocks and mirrors.

Bryne Home Furnishings
3516 W. Magnolia Blvd.
Burbank, CA 91505
(800) 660-3516
Call for information and price quotes. 25 to 40 percent savings on furniture, carpeting, draperies, and mattresses. Authorized dealer for Hickory, Century, Waterford and 100 other quality lines.

Calico Corners
203 Gale Ln.
Kennett Square, Pennsylvania 19348
or
4619 Convoy St.
San Diego, CA 82111
(619) 292-1500
Check your yellow pages for a store near you. Decorative-fabric chain that offers fabrics at discounted prices. Fabricates custom drapery, bedspreads, fabric accessories.

Caroline Country Ruffles
420 W. Frandkin Blvd.
Gastonia, NC 28052

(800) 426-1039
$2 for catalog of curtains, jabots, cascades, swags, blouson valances, balloon curtains, bedspreads, comforters, and fabric accessories. Range of fabrics. Satisfaction guaranteed.

Carter Canopies
P.O. Box 808
Troutman, NC 28166
(800) 538-4071
(704) 528-4071 NC residents
Free brochure of custom-made fishnet canopies, dust ruffles, coverlets, and other country items.

Cindy's Corner
109 Freeman's Bridge Rd.
Scotia, NY 12302
(518) 377-6576
$5 for catalog and swatches featuring reasonably-priced, quality quilts and accessories.

Colonial Country Originals, Inc.
P.O. Box 2010
Hanover, MA 02339
(800) 627-2878
$3 for catalog offering reproduction Colonial and Early-American curtains in a range of fabrics.

The Company Store
500 Company Store Rd.
La Crosse, WI 54601-4477
(800) 356-9367
Free information and savings on their line of high-quality down products. Business established in 1911.

Connecticut Curtain Company
Commerce Plaza, Rt. 6
Danbury, CT 06810
(800) 732-4549, (203) 798-1850
$2 for catalog. Save 20 to 40 percent on window treatment hardware. Iron and steel curtain rods, wooden rods, hard-to-fit corner, arched or palladian

rods, holdbacks, swagholders, and basic rods.

Laura Copenhaver Industries, Inc.
P.O. Box 149
Marion, VA 24354
(800) 227-6797
Free color brochure of handmade canopies, coverlets, dust ruffles, and curtains. Available from inventory or custom-made. Satisfaction guaranteed. Business established in 1916.

Country Curtains
Red Lion Inn
Stockbridge, MA 01262
Free 72-page catalog of country-styled curtains in cottons and cotton blends.

Country Decorators
P.O. Box 224
Norwell, MA 02061
(800) 627-2878
Free 24-page color catalog of fabric window treatments.

Decorum
235-237 Commercial St.
Portland, ME 04101
(207) 775-3346
Free information on their line of roll-top desks, file cabinets, antique lamps, bathroom and plumbing fixtures, and hardware.

Designer Secrets
Box 529
Fremont, NE 68025
$2 for catalog. Up to 50 percent savings on window treatments, wallpaper, accessories, fabrics, bedspreads, and furniture.

Dianthus, Ltd.
P.O. Box 870
Plymouth, MA 02362
(508) 747-4179
$4 for catalog of country-classic

curtains and accessories.

Domestications
P.O. Box 40
Hanover, PA 17333-0040
(800) 746-2555
Free 100-page catalog featuring discounted bedroom ensembles, curtains, accessories, and lamps.

Dorothy's Ruffled Originals
6721 Market St.
Wilmington, NC 28405
$4 for catalog of their line of ruffled curtains and fabric accessories in a range of fabrics.

Especially Lace
202 5th St.
West Des Moines, IA 50265
(515) 277-8778
$3.50 for catalog of lace European curtains and valances.

Fabric Shop
120 N. Seneca Ave.
Shippensburg, PA 17257
(800) 233-7012
Send SASE for free information on their collection of decorator, drapery, and upholstery fabrics. They also offer custom-made drapery, top treatments, bedspreads, accessories.

Faith's Lacery
89 W. Main St.
Dundee, IL 60118
$2 for catalog of all types of lace window treatments and accessories.

Alan Ferguson Associates
422 S. Main St.
P.O. Box 6222
High Point, NC 27262
(919) 889-3866
Featuring discounted unique, one-of-a-kind furnishings for both residential and commercial interiors.

Offering upholstery, cabinetry, wood finishes including faux or rich finishes, casegoods, fine art and sculpture, accessories, rugs and carpets, drapery and upholstery fabrics, lamps, wall-coverings, and antiques. Delivery and setup available nationwide.

The Gazebo of New York
127 East 57th St., Dept. CL
New York, NY 10022
$6 for catalog. Large selection of quilts, duvet covers, dust ruffles, curtains, braided and rag rugs, pillows, antique and new wicker pieces, and other hand-crafted accessories.

Virginia Goodwin
Rt. 2, Box 770
Boone, NC 28607
(800) 735-5191
$1 for information on drapery, valances, canopies, bedspreads, and dust ruffles.

Harris Levy, Inc.
278 Grand St.
New York, NY 10002
(800) 221-7750
(212) 226-3102 NY residents
Free information and savings of up to 40 percent off retail on bed, table, and bath linens from all over the world.

Linen & Lace
#4 Lafayette
Washington, MO 63090
(800) 332-LACE
$2 for catalog of imported Scottish lace curtains, Victorian gifts and accessories.

The Linen Source
5401 Hangar Court
Tampa, FL 33631-3151
(800) 431-2620
Free catalog of discounted bedroom ensembles, curtains, accessories, and

rugs. Satisfaction Guaranteed.

London Lace
167 Newbury St.
Boston, MA 02116
(617) 267-3506
$2 for catalog featuring lace window treatments.

Mather's Department Store
31 E. Main St.
Westminster, MD 21157
(410) 848-6410
Free catalog of country-styled curtains, and valances in a range of fabrics.

MDC Direct, Inc.
P.O. 569
Marietta, GA 30061
(800) 892-2083
Free information and samples. Up to 82 percent savings on all types of mini-blinds, wood blinds, pleated, shades, vertical blinds, and Duettes. They also manufacture bedspreads and draperies. Free UPS shipping.

Montgomery Ward Direct
(800) 852-2711
Call for a free catalog featuring discounted prices on bedding and bath ensembles, bedspreads, accessories, curtains, rugs, bedroom, living and family room furniture.

Muckleberry Farms
1240 Lynway Lane
Atlanta, GA 30311
$3 for catalog of their collection of country quilts, wreaths, and accessories.

Nile Valley Textiles
P O. Box 2213
Salisbury MD 21802-2213
(800) 216-5543
Save 40 to 50 percent on 100-percent-cotton Egyptian sheets.

Olde Mill House Shoppe
105 Strasburg Pike
Lancaster, PA 17602
(717) 299-0678
$1 for catalog of braided rugs, country-style handmade furniture, linens, and bathroom accessories.

Pintchik Homeworks
2106 Bath Ave.
Brooklyn, NY 11214
(800) 847-4199
(718) 996-5580 NY residents
Free brochure and blind-order kit. Up to 79 percent savings on mini-blinds. Savings on wallpaper, window treatment hardware and supplies, paint, and floorcoverings. They guarantee the lowest prices. Business established in 1912. Free UPS shipping.

Premier Blind Co.
317 E. Hempstead
Giddings, TX 78942
(800) 441-1288
Free information and color samples. Save on mini and micro blinds, verticals, pleated shades, Duettes, and drapery. Free UPS shipping.

Quality Furniture Market of Lenoir, Inc.
2034 Hickory Blvd., S.W.
Lenoir, NC 28645
Write for information. Discounts on furniture, bedding, linens, accessories, and lamp shades.

The Renovator's Supply
Renovator's Old Mill
Millers Falls, MA 01349
(413) 659-2211
$3 for catalog of reproduction curtains, antique hardware, lighting, rugs, bathroom and plumbing fixtures, and accessories.

Anne Roche Interiors
255 Park Ave.
Worcester, MA 01609
(508) 757-4657
Free information on custom window
treatments.

Rue DE France
78 Thames St.
Newport, RI 02840
(800) 777-0998
$3 for catalog of lace curtains and
accessories.

Seraph
5606 State Rt. 37
Delaware, OH 43015
(614) 369-1817
They offer coordinated window
treatments, bedroom ensembles,
rugs and accessories.

Spiegel Catalog
P.O. Box 6340
Chicago, IL 60680-6340
(800) 345-4500
$3 for catalog. Full range of interior
products, furniture, curtains, draperies,
accessories, rugs, lamps, etc. Many
items discounted or available discounted through subsequent sale catalogs. Satisfaction guaranteed.

Tioga Mill Outlet
200 S. Hartman St.
York, PA 17403
(717) 843-5139
$2 for information featuring drapery,
upholstery, crewel, and all types of
decorator fabrics.

Touch of Class
Order Dept.
1905 N. Van Buren St.
Huntingburg, IN 47542

(800) 457-7456
Free catalog of bedroom and
bathroom ensembles. Bedspreads,
curtains, drapery and fabric accessories, bathroom accessories, lamps,
and miscellaneous related accessories.

Upholstery Fabric Outlet (UFO)
1918 Roosevelt Ave.
National City, CA 92109
(619) 477-9341
or
1120 N. Melrose Dr.
Vista, CA 92083
(619) 941-2345
Discounted source for decorator and
upholstery fabrics, supplies and drapery hardware.

Vintage Valances
P.O. Box 43326
Cincinnati, OH 45243
(513) 561-8665
$10 for catalog and fabric samples for
Victorian- and Greek-styled valances.

WE R Fabrics
Mission Viejo CA (714) 770-4662
or
Solana Beach, CA (619) 755-1175
Discounted source for decorator and
upholstery fabrics. Custom-made
drapery, valances, bedspreads, fabric
accessories, upholstery, and slipcovers.

Fabrics

1502 Fabrics Outlet of High Point
P.O. Box 7551
High Point, NC 27264
(910) 434-2153
Substanial discounts on first-quality
upholstery fabric and drapery fabrics,
including Waverly fabrics. Shipping
available nationwide.

ABC Decorative Fabrics
2410 298 Ave. N
Clearwater FL 34621
(800) 548-3452
First quality, guaranteed lowest prices.
All major companies.

American Discount Wallcoverings
1411 5th Ave.
Pittsburgh, PA 15219
(800) 777-2737
Free brochure. Savings from 15 to 50
percent on wallpaper, window
treatments, and upholstery fabrics.

The Atrium
430 S. Main St.
High Point, NC 27260
(910) 882-5599
Furniture mall of 35 discount
galleries that represent over 650
furniture manufacturers. Offering
all types of furnishings, including:
accessories, Oriental rugs, lamps
and lighting. Call to be directed to
the gallery that carries specific lines
of furnishings. Featuring nationwide
delivery.

Barnes & Barnes Fine Furniture
190 Commerce Ave.
Southern Pines, NC 28387
(800) 334-8174
Send an SASE for free information.
Savings of up to 50 percent on
furniture, decorator fabrics, and
accessories.

Benington's
1271 Manheim Pike
Lancaster, PA 17601
(800) 252-5060
Ask about their new catalog. First-
quality goods. Up to 75 percent savings on wallpaper, wallpaper borders,
and fabrics. Their line of products
include top-brand carpeting and rugs.
Free shipping.

Blind Works
1605 Badger Dr.
Toms River, NJ 08755
(800) 334-8590
Free information. First-quality goods.
All major brands and types of window
coverings. Up to 80 percent off
department store prices on miniblinds,
vertical blinds and Duettes. Decorator
fabrics are available. Free UPS
shipping.

BMI Home Decorating
P.O. Box 25905
Lexington, KY 40524
Free information. Up to 50 percent
savings on decorator fabrics and wall-
coverings.

Boone Fabrics
Highway 421
Colfax, NC 27235
(800) 635-3396
(910) 668-0854 NC residents
Save up to 70% off retail on name-
brand drapery and upholstery fabrics.
First-quality selection. Large selection
in stock.

J.R. Burrows & Co.
P.O. Box 522
Rockland, MA 02370
$5 for catalog. Artsy wallpaper and
fabrics. Carpet period reproductions.

Calico Corners
203 Gale Ln.
Kennett Square, PA 19348
or
4619 Convoy St.
San Diego CA 82111
(619) 292-1500
Check your yellow pages for a location near you. Decorative fabric chain. Sells fabrics at discounted prices. Custom-made drapery, bedspreads, and fabric accessories.

Columbus Coated Fabrics
1280 N. Grant
Columbus, OH 42136
Various types of coated specialty fabrics.

Cutting Corners
13720 Midway Rd., Ste. 200
Dallas, TX 75244
(915) 942-9780
$10 for catalog of decorator and drapery fabrics.

East Carolina Wallpaper Market
1106 Pink Hill Rd.
Kinston, NC 28501
(800) 848-7283
Free information. Up to 35 to 50 percent savings on wallpaper, wallpaper borders, and fabrics.

FDH Decorative-Fabrics Outlet
500 Townsend Ave.
High Point, NC 27263
(910) 889-9313
Save up to 70% or more off retail on in-stock decorative fabric seconds and first-quality upholstery and drapery fabrics in a range of fabrics from contemporary to traditional.

Fabric Barn
3111 E. Anaheim St.
Long Beach, CA 90804
Discounted decorator and drapery fabrics.

Fabric Center
485 Electric Ave.
Fitchburg, MA 01420
(508) 343-4402
$2 for thick catalog of available fabrics. They offer nationally-advertised decorator fabrics at exceptional values ranging from 25 to 50 percent off. They have been in business over 63 years.

The Fabric Outlet
P.O. Box 2417
South Hamilton, MA 01982
(800) 635-9715
Free information on decorator and drapery fabrics.

Fabric Shop
120 N. Seneca Ave.
Shippensburg, PA 17257
(800) 233-7012
Send SASE for free information. Discounted decorator, drapery, and upholstery fabrics. Custom-made drapery, top treatments, bedspreads, accessories.

Fabrics by Phone
P.O. Box 309
Walnut Bottom, PA 17266
(800) 233-7012
$3 for brochure of decorator and drapery fabrics. Custom-made drapery, top treatments, bedspreads, and accessories.

Fabric Wholesalers, Inc.
P.O. Box 20235
Portland, OR 97220
Free information on discounted decorator and drapery fabrics.

Alan Ferguson Associates
422 S. Main St.
P.O. Box 6222

High Point, NC 27262
(919) 889-3866
Featuring discounted unique, one-of-a-kind furnishings for both residential and commercial interiors. Offering upholstery, cabinetry, wood finishes including faux or rich finishes, casegoods, fine art and sculpture, accessories, rugs and carpets, drapery and upholstery fabrics, lamps, wall-coverings, and antiques. Delivery and setup available nationwide.

Gurian Fabrics
276 5th Ave.
New York, NY 10001
(212) 689-9696
$1 for catalog of crewel fabrics.

Hang-It Now Wallpaper Stores
N. Main St.
Archdale, NC 27263
(800) 325-9494
Free information. Up to 30 to 65 percent savings on wallcoverings. Up to 40 percent savings on decorator fabrics.

Harmony Supply Company
P.O. Box 313
Medford, MA 02155
(617) 395-2600
Free information on coordinating wallpaper and fabrics.

Home Fabric Mills, Inc.
882 S. Main St.
P.O. Box 888
Chelshire, CT 06410
(203) 272-3529
Free brochure on range of interior fabrics: drapery, velvets, upholstery, prints, sheers, and antique satins. Custom-made drapery, top treatments, bedspreads, and fabric accessories.

Labours of Love
3760 Old Clayburn Rd.

Abbotsford BC CN V2S 6B7
(604) 853-9132
$2 for catalog of embroideries and laces.

Lee's Mills
2317 Center Ave.
Janesville, WI 53545
(608) 754-0404
Free information on pile fabrics.

Donna Lee's Sewing Center
25234 Pacific Hwy.
South Kent, WA 98032
$4 for catalog of French and English laces, and Swiss embroidery.

Linen & Lace
#4 Lafayette
Washington, MO 63090
(800) 332-LACE
$2 for catalog of imported Scottish lace curtains, Victorian gifts and accessories.

Marlene's Decorative Fabrics
301 Beech St., Dept. 2J
Hackensack, NJ 07601
(800) 992-7325
Free information and discounted prices on first-quality decorator and upholstery fabrics, and trims.

Mill End Store
8300 SE McLoughlin Blvd.
Portland, OR 97202
(803) 236-1234
Free information on discounted decorator and drapery fabrics.

Monterey Mills Outlet Store
P.O. Box 271
1725 E. Delavan Dr.
Janesville, WI 53545
(800) 438-6387, (608) 754-8309
Free information on pile and fake-fur fabrics to use for bedspreads,

accessories, pillows, etc., priced at least 50 percent off retail.

Nationwide Wholesalers
630 Main St.
Hackensack, NJ 07602
(800) 488-WALL
Free information and vertical blind kit. Up to 78 percent savings on wall-coverings, 80 percent on all types of blinds, and up to 60 percent on decor ator fabrics. Savings on decorator fabrics. NJ and NY residents pay sales tax.

North Carolina Textile Sales of High Point, Inc.
108 Interstate Dr.
High Point, NC 27263
Mailing address:
P.O. Box 7382
High Point, NC 27264
(910) 431-3238
Upholstery and drapery-fabric outlet specializing in first-quality goods. Special orders up to 40% off retail. Featuring Kirsch and Graber hardware and Conso trims. Shipping available nationwide.

Nizhonie Fabrics, Inc.
P.O. Box 729
Cortex, CO 81321
(303) 565-7079
Send SASE for free brochure. Silk-screened Indian designs for draperies, upholstery and trims.

Papers Plus
P.O. Box 204
Countryside, IL 60525
(800) 837-8757
Free information. Savings from 35 to 75 percent on wallpaper. Up to 30 percent savings on fabrics.

Quix 1
P.O. Box 5659

Pittsburgh, PA 15207
(800) 487-6773
Up to 60 percent savings on fabrics from any mill or distributor. Over 500 companies represented. Wholesale prices on miniblinds, vertical blinds, and shades.

Robinson's Wallcoverings
225 W. Spring St.
Titusville, PA 16354
(800) 458-2426
$2 for catalog of wallcoverings and decorator fabrics.

Rubin & Green
290 Grand St.
New York, NY 10002
Send SASE for free information on decorator and upholstery fabrics.

Donna Salyers' Fabulous Furs
700 Madison Ave.
Covington, KY 41011
(800) 848-4680
Free information on fake furs and leather.

Gene Sanes & Associates (Since 1931)
1645 Penn Ave.
Pittsburgh, PA 15222
(800) 729-8839
Upholstery and drapery fabrics from all mills and all distributors at the largest discounts anywhere. Uphol-stered cornices built and shipped by U.P.S.

Sanz International, Inc.
P.O. Box 1794
High Point, NC 27261
(919) 886-7630
Send SASE for free information on wallcoverings, decorator fabrics, car-peting, furniture, and lamps. They will meet or beat any quote, give extra quantity discounts and offer advice on

estimating and installations. Free shipping.

Sew Crafty Drapery & Upholstery Outlet

1201 Baker Rd.
High Point, NC 27263
(910) 434-7679
Save 30 to 70% off retail on in-stock drapery and upholstery fabrics. Featur ing contemporary, traditional, small and large prints.

Shama Imports

P.O. Box 2900
Farmington Hills, MI 48018
(313) 478-7740
Free catalog of cotton and wool, hand-embroidered Indian crewel fabrics at a savings of up to 50 percent off retail prices. They also have available bed-spreads, cushion covers, and table-cloths.

Spiegel Catalog

P.O. Box 6340
Chicago, IL 60680-6340
(800) 345-4500
$3 for catalog. Full range of interior products, furniture, curtains, draperies, accessories, rugs, lamps, etc. Many items discounted or available dis-counted through subsequent sale cat-alogs. Satisfaction guaranteed.

G. Street Fabrics

Mail-Order Service
12240 Wilkins Ave.
Rockville, MD 20852
(301) 231-8998
Free catalog of decorator and drapery fabrics.

Tioga Mill Outlet

200 S. Hartman St.
York, PA 17403
(717) 843-5139

$2 for information on drapery, uphol-stery, crewel, and other types of decor-ator fabrics.

The Unique Needle

539 Blossom Wy.
Hayward, CA 94541
(415) 727-9130
$1.50 for brochure of imported Swiss fabrics, embroideries, French laces, and other decorator fabrics.

Upholstery Fabric Outlet (UFO)

1918 Roosevelt Ave.
National City, CA 92109
(619) 477-9341
or
1120 N. Melrose Dr.
Vista, CA 92083
(619) 941-2345
Discounted source for decorator and upholstery fabrics, supplies and drap-ery hardware.

Victorian Treasures

12148 Madison St. NE
Blaine, MN 55434
$3.50 for catalog of imported laces, Swiss embroideries, and fabrics.

Allan Walker Ltd.

3800 Ivy Rd., NE
Atlanta, GA 30305
(404) 233-1926
Free information on imported tapest-ries.

Wallpaperxpress

P.O. Box 4061
Naperville, IL 60567
(800) 288-9979
Free information. Up to 70 percent savings on wallpaper. Up to 25 per-cent savings on decorator fabrics. Up to 60 percent savings on blinds.

**Warren's Interior Design &
Furniture, Inc.**
P.O. Box 33
Prospect Hill, NC 27314
(800) 743-9792
(910) 562-5198 NC residents
Up to 60% off retail on furniture
from the following brands: Bassett,
Clayton Marcus, Flexsteel, Henry-
Link, Hooker, Leathercraft, Link-
Taylor, Sealy Mattresses, White,
and Howard Miller Clocks. Carpet
brands include: Cabin Crafts, Masland,
Philadelphia, and Sun. Fabric and
wallpaper brands include: Greeff,
Payne, and Schumacher. They also
have a large selection of pictures and
accessories.

WE R Fabrics
Mission Viejo, CA (714) 770-4662
or
Solana Beach, CA (619) 755-1175
Discounted source for decorator
and upholstery fabrics. Custom-
made drapery, valances, bedspreads
and fabric accessories, upholstery,
and slipcovers.

Yankee Wallcoverings, Inc.
109 Accord Park Dr.
Norwell, MA 02061
(800) 624-7711
Free information. Savings from 35 to
75 percent on coordinating
wallcoverings and fabrics.

Wallcoverings

$5 Wallcovering Co.
374 Hall St.
Phoenixville, PA 19460
(800) 5-Dollar.
Call for information on discounted wallcoverings. Up to 80 percent savings on custom blinds.

American Blind & Wallpaper Factory
28237 Orchard Lake Rd.
Farmington Hills, MI 48334
(800) 735-5300
Free information. Up to 78 percent savings on wallcoverings, 80 percent savings on mini and micro blinds, 75 percent savings on wood blinds, vertical blinds, custom-made roller shades, and pleated shades. Free UPS shipping.

American Discount Wallcoverings
1411 5th Ave.
Pittsburgh, PA 15219
(800) 777-2737
Free brochure. Savings from 15 to 50 percent on wallpaper, window treatments, and upholstery fabrics.

Laura Ashley
1300 MacArthur Blvd.
Mahwah, NJ 07430
(800) 223-6917
$4 for catalog of English period reproduction window treatments, fabrics, bedspreads, and other accessories.

Benington's
1271 Manheim Pike
Lancaster, PA 17601
(800) 252-5060
Free information. Featuring first-quality goods. Up to 75 percent savings on wallpaper, wallpaper borders and fabrics. Discounts on top-brand rugs and carpets.

Best Discount Wallcoverings
417 Jackson St.
St. Charles, MO 63301
(800) 328-5550
Free information. Savings from 35 to 75 percent on wallcoverings.

BMI Home Decorating
P.O. Box 25905
Lexington, KY 40524
Free information. Up to 50 percent savings on decorator fabrics and wallcoverings.

Bradbury & Bradbury Wallpapers
P.O. Box 155
Benicia, CA 94510
(707) 746-1900
$10 for catalog offering Victorian-period wallpapers, wallpaper borders, friezes, ceiling papers, and wall frills.

J.R. Burrows & Co.
P.O. Box 522
Rockland, MA 02370
$5 for catalog of artsy wallpaper and fabrics. Carpet period reproductions.

Carefree Wallcoverings
23745 Mercantile Rd.
Cleveland, OH 44122
They offer a line of specialty wallcoverings.

The Decorator's Edge, Inc.
509 Randolph St.
Thomasville, NC 27360
(800) 289-5589
(910) 476-1047
Custom window treatments and interiors. Save up to 75% off retail on mini and micro blinds, 70% off on wood blinds, 60% off on vertical blinds, 20 to 40% off on fabrics, 20 to 40% off on wallpaper, 20 to 50% off

on furniture.

Designer Secrets
Box 529
Fremont, NE 68025
$2 for catalog. Up to 50 percent
savings on window treatments, wallpaper, accessories, fabrics, bedspreads,
and furniture.

Direct Wallpaper Express
374 Hall St.
Phoenixville, PA 19460
(800) 336-9255
Save 40 to 72 percent on top brands
of wallpaper and window treatments.
Pattern-identification service.

East Carolina Wallpaper Market
1106 Pink Hill Rd.
Kinston, NC 28501
(800) 8487283
Free information. Up to 35 to 50
percent savings on wallpaper, wallpaper borders, and fabrics.

Factory Paint Store
505 Pond St.
South Weymouth, MA 02190
(617) 331-1200
Free information on window shades,
wallpaper, paint, and lighting fixtures.

Alan Ferguson Associates
422 S. Main St.
P.O. Box 6222
High Point, NC 27262
(919) 889-3866
Featuring discounted unique, one-
of-a-kind furnishings for both residential and commercial interiors.
Offering upholstery, cabinetry, wood
finishes including faux or rich finishes,
casegoods, fine art and sculpture,
accessories, rugs and carpets, drapery
and upholstery fabrics, lamps, wallcoverings, and antiques. Delivery
and setup available nationwide.

Hang-It Now Wallpaper Stores
N. Main St.
Archdale, NC 27263
(800) 325-9494
Free information. Up to 30 to 65
percent savings on wallcoverings, and
up to 40 percent savings on decorator
fabrics.

Harmony Supply Company
P.O. Box 313
Medford, MA 02155
(617) 395-2600
Free information on coordinating
wallpaper and fabrics.

Headquarters Windows & Walls
8 Clinton Pl.
Morristown, NJ 07960
(800) 338-4882
Free information. Up to 80 percent
savings on micro and miniblinds,
Duettes, wood blinds, vertical blinds,
pleated shades, and toppers and up to
81 percent savings on wallpaper. Free
shipping.

Home Fashion Center
R.R.2, Box 344A
Columbia, MO 65201-9802
Discounts up to 50 percent on
wallcoverings, window blinds,
carpet, and floorcoverings.

Imperial Wallcoverings
23645 Mercantile
Cleveland, OH 44122
Write for quotes. They offer discounts
on all types of wallcoverings.

Nationwide Wholesalers
630 Main St.
Hackensack, NJ 07602
(800) 488-WALL
Free information and vertical-blind kit.
Up to 78 percent savings on wallcoverings, 80 percent on all types of
blinds, and 60 percent savings on

fabrics. NJ an NY residents pay sales tax.

National Blind and Wallpaper Factory
400 Galleria, #400
Southfield, MI 48034
(800) 477-8000
They've merged with Style Wallcovering and Mary's Wallpaper to become the largest mail order discounter, bringing you unbeatable buying power! Up to 80 percent off all name brands with free shipping within 48 hours! Free blind-sample kit.

Number One Wallpaper
2914 Long Beach Rd.
Oceanside, NY 11572
(800) 423-0084
(516) 678-4445 NY residents
Free information on discounted wallpaper. They have over 100,000 rolls in stock. Up to 80 percent savings. Free delivery.

The Paper Place Interiors
606 Idol Dr.
P.O. Box 5985
High Point, NC 27262
(910) 869-8752
$3 for information. Discount prices on 200 lines of name-brand wallcoverings, fabrics, blinds, shades, and woven woods. Including Del Mar window coverings, Dapha furniture, Marbro lamps, and Masland carpet.

Papers Plus
P.O. Box 204
Countryside, IL 60525
(800) 837-8757
Free information. Savings from 35 to 75 percent on wallpaper, up to 30 percent savings on fabrics.

Peerless Wallpaper
39500 14 Mile Rd.

Walled Lake, MI 48390
(800) 999-0898
Up to 75 percent savings on wallpaper. The more you buy, the more you save. Business established over 50 years. 45-day return policy.

Pintchik Homeworks
2106 Bath Ave.
Brooklyn, NY 11214
(800) 847-4199
(718) 996-5580 NY residents
Free brochure and blind-order kit. Wallpaper, window treatment hardware and supplies, paint, and floorcoverings. They guarantee the lowest prices! Business established in 1912.

Post Wallcovering Distributors, Inc.
2065 Franklin Rd.
Bloomfield Hills, MI 48013
(800) 521-0650
Free information. Up to 75 percent off retail on wallcoverings and blinds. Fast, free delivery.

Robinson's Wallcoverings
225 W. Spring St.
Titusville, PA 16354
(800) 458-2426, (814) 827-1893
$2 for catalog of wallcoverings and decorator fabrics. Business established over 72 years ago.

Sanz International, Inc.
P.O. Box 1794
High Point, NC 27261
(919) 886-7630
Send SASE for free information on over 5,000 wallcoverings and borders, decorator fabrics, carpeting, furniture, and lamps. They will meet or beat any quote, give extra-quantity discounts and offer advice on estimating and installations. Free shipping.

Shopright Wallcoverings
P.O. Box 24513
St. Louis, MO 63141
(800) 622-9927
Free information on their line of
wallcoverings.

Silver's Wholesale Club
3001 Kensington Ave.
Philadelphia, PA 19134
(800) 426-6600, (215) 426-7600
Free information. Savings from 30 to
81 percent off retail on first-quality
wallcoverings, borders, brand name
fabrics, blinds, and verticals. Free
delivery.

Smart Wallcoverings
P.O. Box 2206
Southfield, MI 48037
(800) 677-0200
Free information. Up to 50 percent
savings on wallcoverings. They guarantee the lowest prices. Free UPS
shipping.

Smartn'up Wallpaper Outlet
579 Huffman Rd.
Burlington, NC 27215
(910) 584-9131
Savings of up to 80% on brand-
name in-stock wallpaper. Over
10,000 rolls in stock. Shipping
available nationwide. Large
selection of borders, tools, and
accessories.

Southern Discount Wall Covering
1583 N. Military Trail
West Palm Beach, FL 33409
(800) 699-WALL
Up to 80 percent off list on first-
quality name-brand wallcoverings. Free
delivery.

Spiegel Catalog
P.O. Box 6340
Chicago, IL 60680-6340

(800) 345-4500
$3 for catalog. Full range of interior
products, furniture, curtains, draperies,
accessories, rugs, lamps, etc. Many
items discounted or available discounted through subsequent sale
catalogs. Satisfaction guaranteed.

Stencils & Seams Unlimited
RR 2, Box 2377
Raymond, ME 04071
(207) 655-3952
$2.50 for catalog of wallpaper
borders and stenciled valances.

**U.S.A. National
Wholesale Wallcovering**
Rte. 10
Ledgewood, NJ 07852
(800) 631-9341
Free information. Lowest direct-to-
consumer wholesale prices on wallcoverings. 1,000,000 satisfied customers! Free delivery anywhere
in the U.S.A.

United Wallcoverings
23645 Mercantile
Cleveland, OH 44122
Send for information. Discounted
prices on all types of wallcoverings.

Valley Forge Wallpaper
344 Hall St.
Phoenixville, PA 19460
(800) 548-1558
(800) 332-Wall, PA residents
Free information. Up to 40 percent
savings on wallpaper.

Victorian Collectibles
845 E. Glennbrook Rd.
Milwaukee, WI 53217
(414) 352-6971
$3 for brochure of 19th-century
period reproductions of wallpaper and
matching tiles.

Wallpaper Outlet
337 Rt. 46
Rockaway, NJ 07866
(800) 291-WALL
Up to 80 percent off wallpaper. Free
delivery.

Wallpapers Unlimited
P.O. Box 113
La Fox, IL 60147
(800) 228-0355
Free information. Up to 70 percent
savings on wallpaper.

Wallpaperxpress
P.O. Box 4061
Naperville, IL 60567
(800) 288-9979
Free information. Up to 70 percent
savings on wallpaper, up to 25 percent
savings on decorator fabrics, up to 60
percent savings on blinds.

**Warren's Interior Design
& Furniture, Inc.**
P.O. Box 33
Prospect Hill, NC 27314
(800) 743-9792
(910) 562-5198 NC residents
Up to 60% off retail on furniture
from the following brands: Bassett,
Clayton Marcus, Flexsteel, Henry-
Link, Hooker, Leathercraft, Link-
Taylor, Sealy Mattresses, White,
and Howard Miller Clocks. Carpet

brands include: Cabin Crafts, Masland,
Philadelphia, and Sun. Fabric and
wallpaper brands include: Greeff,
Payne, and Schumacher. They also
have a large selection of pictures and
accessories.

Window Express
32525 Stephenson Hwy.
Madison Heights., MI 48071
(800) 772-1947, (800)777-7747
Savings on miniblinds and verticals.

Super savings on wallpaper. Free
shipping for most items.

Yankee Wallcoverings, Inc.
109 Accord Park Dr.
Norwell, MA 02061
(800) 624-7711
Free information. Savings from 35 to
75 percent on coordinating wallcoverings and fabrics.

Yorktowne Wallpaper Outlet
2445 S. Queen St.
York, PA 17402
(800) 847-6142
Free information. Savings from 30 to
70 percent on wallcoverings.

Carpeting, Rugs, Wood Flooring
and Floorcoverings

800 Carpets, Inc.
3017 Third Ave.
Brooklyn, NY 11209
(800) CARPETS
$6 for catalog of braided rugs and
Orientals, both imported and domestic, at low wholesale prices. Business
established in 1932. 100-percent-
satisfaction guaranteed. All domestic
broadloom carpeting available at
wholesale prices. Free shipping.

Abingdon Rug Outlet
246 W. Main St.
Abingdon, VA 24210
(703) 628-9821
Send SASE for free information. Up
to 70 percent savings on handmade
rugs.

Access Carpet
P.O. Box 1007
3068 N. Dug Gap Rd.
Dalton, GA 30722
(800) 848-7747, Ext. 79
Low prices on most major brands of
carpeting.

Adams & Swett
964 Massachusetts Ave.
Boston, MA 02118
(617) 268-8000
$2 for catalog of Early-American
and contemporary hand- and
machine-braided wool rugs.

American Blind &
Wallpaper Factory
28237 Orchard Lake Rd.
Farmington Hills, MI 48334
(800) 735-5300
Call to see what floorcoverings are
available and for free information.
Up to 78 percent savings on

wallcoverings. Up to 80 percent
savings on mini and micro blinds,
75 percent on wood blinds, vertical
blinds, custom-made roller shades,
and pleated shades. Free UPS
shipping.

American Broadloom Braided Rug &
Furniture Company
404 Roosevelt Ave.
Central Falls, RI 02863
(401) 722-2017
Free information on collection of
handmade braided-wool rugs.

Arkansas Oak Flooring
P.O. Box 7227
Pine Bluff, AR 71611
Write for quotes and discounted
prices on oak flooring.

Arizona Mail Order
(800) 362-8415
$2 for Home Etc. catalog featuring
discounted prices on all types of
bedding and bath ensembles, bedspreads, quilts, linens, accessories,
curtains, and rugs.

Armstrong World Industries
P.O. Box 3001
Lancaster, PA 17604
(800) 233-3823
Free information on rugs and
carpets.

Artesanos
222 Galisteo St., Drawer G
Sante Fe, NM 87501
Send for information on their line of
natural-clay tile.

At Home in the Valley
P.O. Box 7303

Van Nuys, CA 91409
(818) 780-4663
$1 for catalog of braided rugs, chair pads, placemats, and curtains.

The Atrium
430 S. Main St.
High Point, NC 27260
(910) 882-5599
Furniture mall of 35 discount galleries that represent over 650 furniture manufacturers. Offering all types of furnishings, including: accessories, Oriental rugs, lamps and lighting. Call to be directed to the gallery that carries specific lines of furnishings. Featuring nationwide delivery.

Aunt Philly's Toothbrush Rugs
P.O. Box 36335
Denver, CO 80236
$2 for catalog of rug-making supplies for constructing rugs from scrap materials.

Authentic Pine Floors, Inc.
P.O. Box 260
Locust Grove, GA 30248
(800) 283-6038
Heart pine and wide plank pine in lengths up to 12".

The Barn
P.O. Box 25
Lehman, PA 18627
(800) 836-5744
They offer custom washable, cotton rag rugs.

Beaver Carpets
697 Varnell Rd.
Dalton, GA
(800) 633-5238
Save 30 to 60 percent on hardwood floors and tiles.

Benington's
1271 Manheim Pike
Lancaster, PA 17601
(800) 252-5060
Ask about their new catalog. First-quality goods of name-brand carpet and rugs. Up to 75 percent savings on wallpaper. Free shipping.

Betsy Bourdon, Weaver
Scribner Hill
Wolcott, VT 05680
(802) 472-6508
$3 for brochure on rugs, handwoven blankets and linens.

Blackwelder's
U.S. Hwy. 21 North
Stateville, NC 28677
(800) 438-0201, (704) 872-8922
$7.50 for catalog. Savings from 30 to 50 percent on office and home furniture, Oriental rugs, carpeting, lamps, etc.

Broad-Axe Beam Co.
Rd. 2, P.O. Box 417
Brattleboro, VT 05301
(802) 257-0064
$2 for brochure offering wide pine flooring of hand-hewn beams.

Bryne Home Furnishings
3516 W. Magnolia Blvd.
Burbank, CA 91505
(800) 660-3516
Call for information and prices. 25 to 40 percent savings on furniture, carpeting, draperies, and mattresses. Authorized dealer for Hickory, Century, Waterford, and 100 other quality lines.

J.R. Burrows & Co.
P.O. Box 522
Rockland, MA 02370
$5 for catalog of special-order,

period carpet reproductions. Artsy wallpaper and fabrics.

Cabistan Oriental Imports
P.O. Box 1951
Dalton, GA 30722
(800) 252-6612
Handmade and machine-made wool area, Oriental, and braided rugs.

Cameo Carpets
Dalton, GA 30722
(800) 343-4914
Free information. Up to 50 percent savings on vinyl flooring and carpeting.

Capel Mill Outlet
Department S. G.
121 E. Main St.
Troy, NC 27371
(910) 576-3211
or
8000 Winchester Dr.
Raleigh, NC 27514
(910)881-0688
Buy direct from the mill and get substantially more on domestic and imported rugs, ranging from small to large. Selection includes over 10,000 rugs, including: traditional wool Orientals, braided, woven and flatweaves, hand-hooked, hand-knotted, contemporary, and Dhurries. Shipping available nationwide.

Capel, Inc.
831 N. Main St.
Troy, NC 27371
They offer a collection of braided rugs.

Carlisle Restoration Lumber, Inc.
HRC 32, P.O. Box 679
Stoddard, NH 03464-9712
(603) 446-3937
They have a line of traditional wide-plank flooring, including Eastern white pine, Southern yellow pine, heart pine, hardwoods, wide oak. Installation available nationwide. 28 years of quality service.

Carpet Express
915 Market St.
Dalton, GA 30720
(800) 922-5582
They claim unequaled value on carpeting. Also, save on Armstrong, Congoleum, Mannington, Tarkett vinyl, and Bruce hardwood flooring.

Carpet Outlet
P.O. Box 417
Miles City, MT 59301
(800) 225-4351
(800) 233-0208 MT residents
Free information and savings on carpets and rugs.

Carpetland
P.O. Box 4405
Rocky Mount, NC 27803-0405
(800) 537-RUGS
Free catalog. Save 40 percent on Karastan Oriental-design rugs. Free shipping.

Carpets, Inc.
7013 Third Ave.
Brooklyn, NY 11209
(800) CARPETS
Free color brochure. Large discounts on Capel area rugs, and most carpeting. Business established in 1932.

Carpets of Georgia
(800) 444-2259
Up to 70 percent savings on first-quality carpeting. Full manufacturer's warranty.

Casa Blanca
629 Hwy 17 N.
Pawleys Island, SC 29585

Their line includes Capel rugs, Karastan rugs, handmade rugs, and carpets. Free rug padding and shipping.

Central Warehouse Furniture Outlet
2352 English Rd.
High Point, NC 27262
(910) 882-9511
Quality furniture offered at lower prices. Including: living room, bedroom, dining room, and kitchen furniture. Market samples available at substantial savings. Lamps, rugs, accessories, and pictures are also available. Offering worldwide shipping.

Chickasaw Memphis Hardwood Flooring Co.
P.O. Box 7253
Memphis, TN 38107
Send for information. They offer a line of hardwood flooring.

Chinese Carpet Center, Inc.
7903 Kinannon Pl.
Lorton, VA 22079
(703) 550-0222
Free illustrated catalog of quality Chinese rugs at competitive prices. Including hand-hooked, hand-tufted, 70-line, 90-line super, 120-line super, and 160-line Sino-Persian. Every color and design meticulously researched and artfully created.

Classic Carpets
P.O. Box 823
Dalton, GA 30722
(800) 377-0572
Call for quotes and samples of discounted carpets and rugs for residential, commercial, and churches.

Cooke Textile Company
P.O. Box 254
Angola, IN 46703
(219) 665-2201

Send SASE for free information on wool rugs.

Country Braid House
29 Clark Rd.
Tilton, NH 03276
(603) 286-4511
Free information on custom braided-wool rugs.

Country Floors
15 E. 16th St.
New York, NY 10003
Ceramic tile from America and Europe.

Country Manor
Rt. 211
P.O. Box 520
Sperryville, VA 22740
(800) 344-8354
$2 for catalog of kitchen accessories and utensils, hand-woven cotton rugs and carpets.

Country Rugs
RD 1, P.O. Box 99
Kintnersville, PA 18930
(215) 346-7068
Hand-woven cotton and wool rugs.

COUNTRY STORE of Geneva, Inc.
28 James St.
Geneva, IL 60134
(708) 879-0098
$2 for catalog of country-styled tin chandeliers, lamps, accessories, and braided rugs.

Custom Hooked Rugs
RFD 2, P.O. Box 213
Middle Jam Rd.
Sebago Lake, ME 04075
(207) 892-8660
Free information on custom handmade wool rugs.

El Paso Saddleblanket Co.
601 N. Oregon
El Paso, TX 79901
(800) 351-7847, (915) 544-1000
Free catalog of handwoven rugs, woven by Mexican Indians. They also carry wool rugs made in the U.S.A.

Ewesful Crafts-The Yorks
Rt. 1, 1041 7 Mile Rd.
Athens, MI 49011
(517) 741-7949
Free information on handwoven cotton and denim rag rugs.

Family Heir-loom Weavers
RD 3, P.O. Box 59 E
Red Lion, PA 17356
(717) 246-2431
$3 for catalog of historic, patterned carpets.

Alan Ferguson Associates
422 S. Main St.
P.O. Box 6222
High Point, NC 27262
(919) 889-3866
Featuring discounted unique, one-of-a-kind furnishings for both residential and commercial interiors. Offering upholstery, cabinetry, wood finishes including faux or rich finishes, casegoods, fine art and sculpture, accessories, rugs and carpets, drapery and upholstery fabrics, lamps, wallcoverings, and antiques. Delivery and setup available nationwide.

Florida Tile
% Sikes Corp.
Lakeland, FL 33802
Send for information on their line of tile.

Folkheart Rag Rugs
18 Main St.
Bristol, VT 05443
(803) 453-4101
$1 for brochure of cotton stenciled rag rugs.

Furnitureland South, Inc.
Business I-85 at Riverdale Rd.
P.O. Box 1550
High Point, NC 27282
(910) 841-4328
Very large showroom (over 322,000 square feet) of discounted fine furniture and Oriental rugs in gallery settings. Including bedroom, dining room, leather, upholstery, office, outdoor, bedding, accessories, lamps, clocks, Oriental rugs, fine art. The following lines are represented: American Drew, Bernhardt, Broyhill, Century, Clayton Marcus, Cochrane, Drexel Heritage, Hickory-White, Lane, LaBarge, Leathercraft, Lexington, Pulaski, Stanley, Thomasville, and Virginia House. Nationwide shipping and setup.

The Gazebo of New York
127 East 57th St., Dept. CL
New York, NY 10022
$6 for catalog. They offer a large selection of quilts, duvet covers, dust ruffles, curtains, braided and rag rugs, pillows, antique and new wicker pieces, and other handcrafted accessories.

Gold Label Carpet
P. O. Box 3876
Dalton, GA 30719
(800) 346-4531
Low prices on carpeting. Free samples available. Buy mill direct.

F. J. Hakimian, Inc.
136 E. 57th St., Ste. 201
New York, NY 10022
(212) 371-6900
Free information available on their collection of Oriental and European carpets, rugs, and tapestries.

Heirloom Rugs
28 Harlem St.
Rumford, RI 02916
(215) 438-5672
$2 for catalog of hand-hooked rugs.

Heritage Rug Weavers
4241 Sunnyside Drive
P.O. Box 195
Buckingham, PA 18912
(215) 794-3738
Custom rag wool rugs. From
traditional to contemporary designs,
HRW can complement your customers' decor with superior rugs up to
15' X 36'. Free catalog and price list.

High Point Oriental-Rug Gallery
301 N. Main St.
High Point, NC 27260
(910) 889-8958
Collection of discounted quality
hand-knotted Oriental rugs from
Persia, Turkey, Afghanistan,
Pakistan, China, and India.
Shipping available nationwide.

Home Carpet Industries, Inc.
2730 Dug Gap Road, S.W.
P.O. Box 326
Dalton, GA 30722-0326
(800) 542-3226
(706) 277-3322 GA residents
Free samples and product literature.
Save 50 percent or more on more
than 100 styles of residential and
commercial carpet. First-quality carpet.
No minimum order amount.

Home Fashion Center
R.R.2, Box 344A
Columbia, MO 65201-9802
Discounts up to 50 percent on wall-
coverings, window blinds, carpet, and
floorcoverings.

HSS
941 Linda Vista

Mountain View, CA 94043
(800) 637-0477
They offer antique heart-pine flooring.
Prices start at $2.50 per sq. ft. Feat-
uring quarter-sawn oak flooring (no
sanding required) 3" to 8" wide - $3.05
per sq. foot.

IKEA, Inc.
P.O. Box 103016
Roswell, GA 30076-9860
(215) 834-0150
Check your yellow pages or call for
their nearest location and catalog. This
is a chain store offering reasonably
priced Swedish-style furniture, lighting,
flooring, and accessories. Satisfaction
guaranteed.

Interiors of High Point
1701-C N. Main St.
High Point, NC 27262
(800) 999-0520
(910) 887-0520 NC residents
They specialize in home offices and
feature discounted office, contract
furnishings, home furnishings, outdoor
furnishings, Oriental rugs, pictures,
accessories. Over 300 lines represented, including: Flexsteel, Hekman,
Hickory-Fry, Hooker, Lane, Lexington,
Tropitone, and Universal. They offer
nationwide shipping.

Charles W. Jacobsen, Inc.
401 N. Salina St.
Syracuse, NY 13202
(315) 422-7832
Free information on low-priced handwoven Oriental rugs, from mats to
giant carpets. Free shipping. Rugs can
be sent on approval. Business established over 60 years ago.

Johnson's Carpets, Inc.
3239 South Dixie Hwy.
Dalton, GA 30720
(800) 235-1079

(706) 277-2775 GA residents
Free information and free samples on all qualities of carpeting. Up to 80 percent savings on carpet and hand-carved custom area rugs from over 50 mills (choose from over 100 standard patterns or design your own).

K & D Supply Company
1440 Industrial Dr.
Matthews, NC 28105
(800) 477-1400
$3 for catalog of flat-braided rugs.

Kaoud Brothers Oriental Rugs
17 S. Main St.
West Hartford, CT 06107
(203) 233-6211
$5 for catalog of Oriental rugs.

Kentucky Wood Floors
P.O. Box 33276
Louisville, KY 40232
Send for information. They offer a line of wood flooring.

Kimberly Black Rugs and Accessories
P.O. Box 472927
Charlotte, NC 28247
(800) 296-6099, (704) 846-6099
$3 for catalog of large selection of authentic flat-braid and woven flat-weave rugs. Satisfaction guaranteed. Free shipping.

Tom E. Knisely, Handweaver
1785 York Rd.
Dover, PA 17315
(717) 938-9920
Handwoven rugs and fabrics in traditional designs.

Larchmont Woolcrafters
2630 Brannon Rd.
Micholasville, KY 40356
$2 for brochure on hand-hooked rugs.

The Linen Source
5401 Hangar Court
Tampa, FL 33631-3151
(800) 431-2620
Call for a free catalog. Discounted bedroom ensembles, curtains, accessories, and rugs. Satisfaction guaranteed.

Long's Carpet, Inc.
2625 S. Dixie Hwy.
Dalton, GA 30720
(800) 545-5664, Ext. 44
Up to 70 percent savings on name-brands of carpeting.

Mills River
713 Old Orchard Rd.
Hendersonville, NC 28739
(800) 874-4898
$2 for catalog of flat-braided rugs, bird houses, and decorative accessories for various holidays.

Missouri Hardwood Flooring Co.
114 N. Gay
St. Louis, MO 63105
Send for information on available hardwood flooring.

Montgomery Ward Direct
(800) 852-2711
Call for a free catalog featuring discounted prices on bedding and bath ensembles, bedspreads, accessories, curtains, rugs, bedroom, living and family room furniture.

Claire Murray, Inc.
P.O. Box 1089
North Charlestown, NH 03603
(800) 252-4733
$5 for catalog featuring hand-hooked rugs.

National Carpet
1384 Coney Island Ave.
Brooklyn, NY 11230

$3 for catalog of first-quality repro-
duction Turkish, Persian, Oriental, Hungarian, Colonial, braided, and
hand-hooked rugs. Up to 80 percent
savings off retail.

Nemo Tile Co.
48 E. 21st. St.
New York, NY 10010
Send for brochures and pricing on
their line of tile.

Network Floor Covering
3200 Dug Gap Rd.
Dalton, GA 30720
(800) 442-2013, Ext. 90
Free brochures, quotes, and
samples. Up to 80 percent savings
on first-quality carpet. Quotes on all
national brands. Business established
in 1970.

Olde Mill House Shoppe
105 Strasburg Pike
Lancaster, PA 17602
(717) 299-0678
$1 for catalog of braided rugs, coun-
try-style handmade furniture, linens,
bathroom accessories.

The Paper Place Interiors
606 Idol Dr.
P.O. Box 5985
High Point, NC 27262
(910) 869-8752
$3 for information. Discount prices
on 200 lines of name-brand wallcoverings, fabrics, blinds, shades, and
woven woods. Including Del Mar
window coverings, Dapha furniture,
Marbro lamps, and Masland carpet.

Paradise Mills
P.O. Box 2488
Dalton, GA 30722
(800) 338-7811
Call or write for free carpet samples
(residential and commercial), buyer's

guide and price quotes. Up to 80
percent savings on carpet, designer
rugs, vinyl, or hardwood flooring. They
offer a manufacturer's 10-year
warranty.

Peerless Imported Rugs
3033 N. Lincoln Ave.
Chicago, IL 60657
(800) 621-6573
$11 for catalog. Handmade and
machine-made Oriental rugs,
Navajo, Colonial braided, and
European tapestries.

Pennwood
P.O. Box 180
East Berlin, PA 17316
Send for information on hardwood
flooring.

**Pennsylvania House Collectors'
Gallery of High Point**
P.O. Box 6437
1300 North Main St.
High Point, NC 27262
Mailing address:
P.O. Box 6437
High Point, NC 27262
(910) 887-3000
Clearance center with discounts of up
to 50% on living-room, bedroom,
dining-room, upholstery, leather
furniture, bedding, rugs, entertainment
units, lamps, and accessories. Pennsylvania House and other interior
furnishings. They ship nationwide.

Pintchik Homeworks
2106 Bath Ave.
Brooklyn, NY 11214
(800) 847-4199
(718) 996-5580 NY residents
Free brochure and order-kit for
wallpaper, window-treatment
hardware and supplies, paint, and
floorcoverings. They guarantee the

lowest prices. Business established in 1912.

Quality Discount Carpet
1207 W. Walnut Ave.
Dalton, GA 30720
(800) 233-0993
(404) 226-7611 GA residents
Free information. Up to 50 percent savings on carpeting.

Rastetter Woolen Mill
5802 Star Rt. 39
Millersburg, OH 44654
(216) 674-2103
Free information on rag rugs, area rugs, stair runners, and carpeting.

Rave Carpet, Inc.
2875 Cleveland Rd.
Dalton, GA 30721
(800) 942-6969, Ext. 75
Savings on Stainmaster and other carpets.

The Renovator's Supply
Renovator's Old Mill
Millers Falls, MA 01349
(413) 659-2211
$3 for catalog of reproduction antique hardware, lighting, bathroom and plumbing fixtures, accessories, and curtains.

Rug Factory Store
560 Mineral Spring Ave.
P.O. Box 249
Pawtucket, RI 02860
(401) 724-6840
$2 for catalog of braided rugs, bordered area rugs, Scandinavian, Early American, and traditional rugs.

The Rug Store
2201-F Crown Point Executive Dr.
Charlotte, NC 28227
(800) 257-5078

$5 for 48-page catalog. Save 33 to 50 percent on fine-quality area rugs.

S & S Mills Carpet
2650 Lakeland Rd.
Dalton, GA 30720
(800) 241-4013
Call for information and a free video. $5 for carpet-sample books. Savings of 50 percent on carpeting. Delivery usually within one week.

Sanz International, Inc.
P.O. Box 1794
High Point, NC 27261
(919) 886-7630
Send SASE for free information of wallcoverings, decorator fabrics, carpeting, furniture, and lamps.

Southern Rug
2325 Anderson Rd.
Crescent Springs, KY 41017
(800) 541-RUGS
$5 for catalog of handmade, flat-braided rugs in wool blends.

Southern Rug-Home Shopping
6822 22nd Ave. North, Unit 124
St. Petersburg, FL 33702
(813) 847-3894
$5 for catalog of Oriental and braided rugs.

Spiegel Catalog
P.O. Box 6340
Chicago, IL 60680-6340
(800) 345-4500
$3 for catalog. Full range of interior products, furniture, curtains, draperies, accessories, rugs, lamps, etc. Many items discounted or available discounted through subsequent sale catalogs. Satisfaction guaranteed.

Stone River
P.O. 724
Morgan Town, KY 42261

(502) 526-2824
Featuring wide-plank traditional poplar hardwood flooring at affordable prices.

Stylemark Carpet Mills Inc.
3358 Capitol Dr.
Dalton, GA 30720
(800) 532-2257
Free sample folders. Residential and commercial carpeting. Save 50 percent or more on carpeting.

Sunbelt Flooring Brokers, Inc.
P.O. Box 45063
Baton Rouge, LA 70895
(800) 749-1804
Free information. Up to 50 percent savings on carpeting and vinyl floor coverings.

Sykes Flooring Co.
P.O. Box 999
Warren, AR 71671
Send for information on their line of specialty flooring.

Tab Oriental Rugs & Crafts
100-118 S. Main St.
High Point, NC 27260
(910) 885-1463
Specializing in Pakistani rugs at wholesale prices. Shipping available nationwide.

Tilemart
2465 S. M-139
Baton Harbor, MI 49022
(616) 925-0629
They offer free samples of closeout tiles and prefinished wood flooring.

Timberknee Ltd.
1 L Street
Randolph, VT 05060
(802) 728-9823
Traditional pine and hardwood flooring.

Traditional Country Crafts, Inc.
P.O. Box 111
Landisville, PA 17538
$1 for brochure on hand-loomed rag rugs.

Trott Furniture Company
P.O. Box 7
Richlands, NC 28574
(800) 682-0095
$5 for catalog featuring Oriental rugs, 18th-century mahogany, walnut and cherry furniture.

Upton's Carpet & Rug Gallery
781 N. Main St.
High Point, NC 27260
(910) 886-4937
Specializing in rugs and carpets, including: American Showcase, Couristan, Karastan, Lydian, Mastlan, Milliken, and imported rugs.

Village Carpet
1114 Conover Blvd., West
Conover, NC 28613
Free information and up to 50 percent savings on carpeting.

Wall Furniture Company's Karastan Carpet & Rug Center
(800) 877-1955
(919) 852-9573 NC residents
Substantial savings on Karastan rugs of all sizes and styles.

Warehouse Carpets, Inc.
P.O. Box 3233
Dalton, GA 30721
(800) 526-2229
(404) 226-2229 GA residents
Free information. Up to 40 percent savings on brand name rugs and carpeting.

Warren's Interior Design &- Furniture, Inc.
P.O. Box 33

Prospect Hill, NC 27314
(800) 743-9792
(910) 562-5198 NC residents
Up to 60% off retail on furniture
from the following brands: Bassett,
Clayton Marcus, Flexsteel, Henry-
Link, Hooker, Leathercraft, Link-
Taylor, Sealy Mattresses, White, and
Howard Miller Clocks. Carpet brands
include: Cabin Crafts, Masland,
Philadelphia, and Sun. Fabric and
wallpaper brands include: Greeff,
Payne, and Schumacher. They also
have a large selection of pictures and
accessories.

Weavery
Harriet Giles
2305 Delong Rd.
Lexington, KY 40515
(606) 272-1910
Free information on traditional and
contemporary handwoven cotton
and wool rag rugs.

A. West & Co.
P.O.1086
Dalton, GA 30722
(800) 247-3707
Guaranteed lowest prices nationwide.
Specify brand, style, and color for
quotes.

Thomas K. Woodard
American Antiques & Quilts
835 Madison Ave.
New York, NY 10021
(212) 988-2906
$5 for catalog of Early-American area
rugs and runners.

Woodhouse
P.O. Box 7336
Rocky Mountain, NC 27804
(919) 977-7336
$5 for brochure, and $25 for sample
kit of wide, country-plank or elegant
quarter-sawn plank flooring. Includes

antique heart pine, oak, and special
hardwoods at reasonable prices. Prefinished or unfinished.

Yankee Pride
29 Parkside Circle, Dept. L14
Braintree, MA 02184
(617) 848-7610
$3 for 56-page color catalog featuring
wool braided and hooked rugs, Oriental and round rugs, Dhurries, ready
made and custom made. Complete
selection of chair pads, runners,
braided stair treads, etc.

York Interiors, Inc.
2821 E. Prospect Rd.
York, PA 17402
(800) 723-7029
Free information on Oriental rugs.

Zaki Oriental Rugs
1634 N. Main St.
High Point, NC 27262
(910) 884-4407
Large showroom featuring Oriental
rugs from Afghanistan, China, Pakistan, India, Turkey, and Iran. Dhurries
from India and Kilims from China,
Romania, and Turkey. Shipping
available nationwide.

Table Pads

Guardian Custom Products
P.O. Box A
LaGrange, IN 46761
(800) 444-0778, Ext. 600
(800) 668-7439 Canadian residents
Free information on custom table
pads. Free kit available. They offer a
Lifetime-and-a-Day Guarantee.
Business established in 1923.

Factory-Direct Table Pad Co.
1501 W Market St.
Indianapolis, IN 46222
(800) 428-4567
Free information. Up to 70 percent
savings on custom table pads. 20-year
guarantee.

Pioneer Table Pad
P.O. Box 449
Gatesmill, OH 44040-9901
(800) 541-0271
Free brochure on low-priced, fine
traditional, hand-tailored table
padding. Family-owned business,
established over 75 years ago.

Sentry Table-Pad Co.
1170 Stella St.
St. Paul, MN 55108
(800) 328-7237, ext. 210
Free information. Custom table pads.
15-year guarantee. Business established in 1911.

Furniture

American Folk Art
354 Kennesaw
Marietta, GA 30060
Featuring handmade willow furniture.

American Furniture Galleries
P.O. Box 60
Montgomery, AL 36101
(800) 547-5240
$1 for brochure of handcrafted
reproduction-Victorian furniture.

American Furniture Outlet
2020 W. Green Dr.
High Point, NC 27260
(800) 766-1782
(910) 882-4045 NC residents
Specializing in discounted leather
furniture and furniture for living
rooms, dining rooms, bedrooms,
recliners, entertainment centers,
wicker, curios, and clocks. Brands
include: American Drew, Bassett,
Broyhill, Emerson Leather, Flexsteel,
Formal Leather, Hickorycraft, Hooker,
Howard Miller, Lexington, Old Salem,
Peoploungers, Pulaski, Riverside,
Stanton Cooper, Temple Stuart,
Universal, and Woodmark. Nationwide
delivery and setup available.

American Starbuck
P.O. Box 15376, Dept. CL0194
Lenexa, KS 66215
(913) 894-1567
Send for free catalog on low-priced
and quality-constructed pencil-post
beds, trundle beds, and rope beds.
Free shipping in U.S.A.

Amish Country Collection
Sunset Valley Rd., RD 5
New Castle, PA 16105
(800) 232-6474

Line of Amish-styled hickory and oak
furniture. They also have available
Amish rugs, fabric accessories, and
crafts.

Anderson Bedroom Organizer
(800) 782-4825
Call for information on their line of
space-saving bedroom organizers.

Angel House Designs
R.F.D. 1 Box 1, Rt. 148
Brookfield, MA 01506
(508) 867-2517
$3 for information and fabric swatches
of traditional and country-styled
upholstered furniture.

Annex Furniture Gallery
P.O. Box 958
High Point, NC 27260
Featuring all types of discounted
furniture.

Antiquarian
60 Dartmouth St.
Springfield, MA 01109
(413) 781-6927
$4 for catalog of reproductions of
Victorian furniture and accessories.

Arts by Alexander
701 Greensboro Rd.
High Point, NC 27260
(910) 884-8062
Featuring unusual name-brand
contemporary, traditional, and
Oriental-styled furniture, accessories,
art and framing. Nationwide delivery
available. Business established 50
years.

The Atrium
430 S. Main St.
High Point, NC 27260
(910) 882-5599

Furniture mall of 35 discount galleries that represent over 650 furniture manufacturers. Offering all types of furnishings, including: accessories, Oriental rugs, lamps and lighting. Call to be directed to the gallery that carries specific lines of furnishings. Featuring nationwide delivery.

Backwood 14 Furnishings
Rt. 28, P.O. Box 161
Indian Lake, NY 12842
(518) 251-3327
Free information on rustic-styled beds, desks, tables, and chairs.

Ballard Designs
1670 DeFoor Ave. NW
Atlanta, GA 30318
(404) 351-5099
$3 for catalog on furniture, fabric, and cast decorative accessories for interiors and exteriors.

Barnes & Barnes Fine Furniture
190 Commerce Ave.
Southern Pines, NC 28387
(800) 334-8174
Send a SASE for free information on over 100 lines of discounted furniture, representing savings of up to 50 percent on furniture, decorator fabrics, and accessories.

Robert Barrow Furniture Maker
412 Thames Ave.
Southern Pines, NC 02809
(401) 253-4434
$3 for catalog of handmade Windsor chairs.

C.H. Becksvoort
P.O. Box 12
New Gloucester, ME 04260
(207) 926-4608
$5 for catalog of handmade cherry

furniture and accessories in traditional, Shaker, or contemporary styles.

Bedroom Furniture and Mattress Discounters
2020 S. Main St.
High Point, NC 27260
(910) 889-7378
Discounted prices on water mattresses and bedroom furniture. Nationwide delivery available.

Bennington Furniture Gallery
1300 S. Main St.
High Point, NC 27262
(910) 884-1894
Tremendous savings on fine solid wood, period furniture from hundreds of American manufacturers. Specializing in country and Shaker reproductions. Offering nationwide shipping.

Best Furniture Distributors
16 W. Main
P.O. Box 489
Thomasville, NC 27360
(800) 334-8000
Free information and savings of up to 40 percent on furniture and accessories.

Big Country
242 Long John Silver Dr.
Wilmington, NC 28405
(800) 344-4072
Free information on handmade wood furniture reproductions.

Blackwelder's
U.S. Hwy. 21 North
Stateville, NC 28677
(800) 438-0201, (704) 872-8922
$7.50 for catalog. Savings from 30 to 50 percent on office and home furniture, Oriental rugs, carpeting, lamps, etc.

The Bombay Co.
P.O. Box 161009
Fort Worth, TX 76161-1009
(800) 829-7789
Call for free catalog and nearest
location. Over 390 locations in the
U.S. and Canada. Featuring reasonably-priced traditional and Oriental
furniture, and accessories.

Bonita Furniture Galleries
Rt. 5, P.O. Box 105
U.S. Hwy 321 North
Hickory, NC 28601
(704) 396-3178
Free information on their line of
furniture and accessories.

**Bowen Town & Country
Furniture Co.**
4805 Shattalon Dr.
Winston-Salem, NC 27106
(910) 924-9311
or
1910 Mooney St.
Winston-Salem, NC 27103
(910) 765-1360
Discount prices on over 200 lines of
furniture, including: bedroom, dining
room, upholstery, occasional, accessories, office furniture, outdoor furniture, wicker, leather, dinettes, bedding, lamps, fine art. Available brands
include: Action, Broyhill, Craftique,
Hancock & Moore, Hekman, Henkel-
Harris, Knob Creek, Laine, Lane,
Lexington, Sealy, Sligh, Stanley,
Statton, and Taylor-King. Business
established 1956. Nationwide delivery
and setup available.

Boyles Distinctive Furniture
727 N. Main St.
High Point, NC 27261
(910) 889-4147
or
616 Old Greensboro Rd.
High Point, NC 27260

(910) 884-8088
Featuring over 100 lines of fine
furniture discounted up to 50% off
retail. Including bedroom, dining
room, upholstered furniture, leather,
occasional, office, outdoor, bedding,
lamps, and accessories. Lines include:
Baker, Bernhardt, Century, Councill,
Drexel Heritage, Hancock & Moore,
Henkel-Harris, Henredon, Hickory,
Hickory Chair, Kingsdown, LaBarge,
Sherrill, Southwood, Statton, Sterns &
Foster, and Thomasville. Business
established 40 years.

Brass Beds, Direct
4866 W. Jefferson Blvd.
Los Angeles, CA 90016
(800) 727-6865
Free information and discounted
prices on brass beds. Business
established over 21 years ago.

Brentwood Manor Furnishings
316 Virginia Ave.
Clarksville, VA 23927
(800) 225-6105
Free information and factory-direct
prices on furniture, window treatments, draperies, accessories, and
clocks and mirrors.

Bryne Home Furnishings
3516 W. Magnolia Blvd.
Burbank, CA 91505
(800) 660-3516
Call for information and prices. 25 to
40 percent savings on furniture,
carpeting, draperies, and mattresses.
Authorized dealer for Hickory,
Century, Waterford, and 100 other
quality lines.

**Curtis Buchanan,
Windsor Chairmaker**
208 E. Main St.
Jonesborough, TN 37659
(617) 753-5160

$2 for brochure on Windsor chairs.

Michael Camp, Cabinetmaker
495 Amelia
Plymouth, MI 48170
(313) 459-1190
$3 for catalog of custom reproduction
furniture from the 18th and 19th
centuries.

Candlertown Chairworks
P.O. Box 1630
Candler, NC 28715
(704) 667-4844
$2 for catalog featuring country-style
chairs, benches, stools with milk-paint
finish.

Carolina Furniture Gallery
Rt.1, P.O. Box 37A
Thomasville, NC 27360
(919) 475-1309
Free information on their line of
furniture and accessories.

Carolina Interiors
115 Oak Ave.
Kannapolis, NC 28081
(704) 933-1888
$5 for catalog. Savings from 20 to 60
percent on furniture.

Carolina Leather House, Inc.
P.O. Box 5195
Hickory, NC 28601
(704) 322-4478
$2 for catalog offering leather
furniture.

Carolina Sofa Company
7201 Glenwood Ave.
Raleigh, NC 27612
(919) 781-8020
or
6500 E. Independence Blvd.
Charlotte, NC 28212
(704) 535-6300

Factory-direct prices on sofas, loveseats, sleepers, and sectionals in a
large selection of fabrics. Over 25,000
different frames and fabric combinations are available. Shipping available
worldwide.

Cayton Furniture, Inc.
217 W Third St
Washington, NC 27889
(919) 946-4121
Call for quotes and brochure. Guaranteed best buy in NC. Direct in-
home setup since 1958. Member of
Better Business Bureau and NHFA.

Central Warehouse Furniture Outlet
2352 English Rd.
High Point, NC 27262
(910) 882-9511
Quality furniture offered at lower
prices. Including: living room, bedroom, dining room, and kitchen furniture. Market samples available at
substantial savings. Lamps, rugs,
accessories, and pictures are also
available. Offering worldwide shipping.

Cherry & Deen Furniture
1214 Goshen Mill Rd.
Peach Bottom, PA 17563
(717) 548-3254
$2 for brochure of custom traditional
furniture.

Cherry Hill Furniture
P.O. Box 7405
Furnitureland Station
High Point, NC 27264
(800) 888-0933
Free information. $5 for furniture
portfolio. Up to 50 percent savings on
furniture. 500 quality brands. Business
established in 1933.

Class Fab Mica Works
1401 S. 30th Ave.
Hollywood, FL 33020

(305) 945-3351
Free information on their collection of
wall units, desks, dining, bedroom, and
mattresses.

Classic Doors & Mantels
2100 S. Main St.
High Point, NC 27263
(910) 889-3667
or
1-C 2810 Yonkers
Raleigh, NC 27613
(919) 829-0208
Brochures available. Factory-direct
prices on sofas, loveseats, sleepers,
chairs, ottomans, and chaise lounges.
Up to 60% off retail. Selection of over
500 fabrics. Handcrafted doors and
fireplace mantles. Custom-made to
your specifications. Worldwide
shipping available.

Classic Interiors
Livonia, MI 48150
(810) 474-6900
Discounted furniture prices.
Furniture line includes Bob Timber-
lake, Old Salem, American Country
West. Large selection of quality
manufacturers. Free delivery in
Michigan. Credit terms available.

Coffey Furniture Galleries
P.O. Box 141
Granite Falls, NC 28630
(704) 396-2900
Free information on their line of
furniture and accessories.

Cohasset Colonials
271 Ship St.
Cohasset, MA 02025
(617) 383-0110
Featuring reproduction Colonial
furniture. Available assembled,
unfinished, finished or in kit form.
Also, carry lighting fixtures, brass and
pewter accessories.

Colonial Designs Furniture
P.O. Box 1429
Havertown, PA 19083
(215) 446-0835
$2 for catalog of reproduction
Colonial furniture.

Colonial Furniture Shops
P.O. Box 12007
Winston-Salem, NC 27117
(919) 788-2121
$1 for brochure of reproduction
Colonial furniture.

Colonial Williamsburg
P.O. Box 3532
Williamsburg, VA 23187
(800) 446-9240
Reproductions of Colonial furniture
from Williamsburg.

Color-Tex Distributors
1102 Dorris Ave.
P.O. Box 7023
High Point, NC 27264
(800) 442-9049
(910) 886-3516
Call for information on wholesale
prices on name-brand furniture.
Brands include: American Drew,
Bassett, Cochrane, Flexsteel, Hekman,
Hood, Hooker, King Hickory, Kingsdown, Lea, Lexington, Marlow, Nathan Hale, Universal, Virginia House,
and Winston Patio. Offering superior
service and value.

Conrad's Mail Order
475 Oberlin Ave., South
Lakewood, NJ 08701
(508) 772-0023
$2 for catalog of furniture,
kitchenware, fabrics, accessories,
lamps, floorcoverings, wallpaper,
lighting fixtures, and lamps.

Corner Hutch Furniture
(704) 873-1773

Highway 21 North
Statesville, NC 28677
(704) 873-1773
Discount prices on fine home
furnishings including the following
brands: American Drew, Barca-
lounger, Brown-Jordan, Century,
Chapman Lamps, Cochrane, Councill
Craftsman, Craftique, Distinctive
Leather, Emerson Leather, Haber-
sham Plantation, Henry-Link Wicker,
Hickory Chair, Hooker, Howard Mil-
ler, Jamestown Sterling, LaBarge,
Lane, Lexington, Link-Taylor, Nathan
Hale, Pulaski, Sealy, Serta, Stanley,
Stiffel, Swan Brass Beds, Tropitone,
Wellington Hall, and Woodmark
Chairs. Shipping available nationwide.

Cornucopia
P.O. Box 30
Harvard, MA 01451
$2 for catalog of Windsor chairs,
hutches, tables, and settees.

Country Bed Shop
Richards Rd., RR 1
P.O. Box 65
Ashby, MA 01431
$4 for catalog of handmade, repro-
duction Early-American beds, chairs,
and tables.

The Country House
805 E. Main St.
Salisbury, MD 21801
(410) 749-1959
$2 for catalog of their extensive select
ion of Colonial home furnishings.

Country Reproductions
(802) 728-4901
Call for brochure on their line of
handmade Vermont cupboards.

Country Store
P.O. Box 17696

Whitefish Bay, WI 53217
(414) 263-1919
$2 for catalog offering willow
furniture.

Country Workshop
95 Rome St.
Newark, NJ 07105
(800) 526-8001
(201) 589-3407 NJ residents
$1 for catalog of line of wood
furniture. Furniture may be
ordered unfinished or finished.

Crestwood Galleries
P. O. Drawer 745
Linville, NC 28646
(704) 898-6162
Free price quotes on Lexington and
Bob Timberlake furniture. Save from
50 to 60 percent off retail.

Gerald Curry, Cabinetmaker
Pound Hill Rd.
Union, ME 04862
(207) 785-4633
Free information on reproduction
Early-American wood furniture.

**Custom Furniture Corp. of
High Point**
721 S. Hamilton St.
High Point, NC 27260
(910) 885-9431
Made-to-order upholstered furniture
at factory-direct prices. Their line
includes: sofas, loveseats, sleepers,
chairs, accent chairs, and recliners.
Shipping available nationwide.

Frederick Dackloe & Bros., Inc.
P.O. Box 427
Portland, PA 18351
(717) 897-6172
$5 for catalog of Windsor chairs,
rocking chairs, stools, and benches.

Dallas Furniture
215 N. Centennial St.
High Point, NC 27260
(910) 884-5759
Exceptional savings on quality
furniture, bedding, and accessories.
Brands include: American Drew, Bas-
sett, Broyhill, Flexsteel, Hooker, Lane,
Lexington, Lyon Shaw, Pulaski, Singer,
Spring Air Bedding, Strato-lounger,
Temple-Stuart, Universal, and Howard
Miller Clocks. Special orders welcome.
Nationwide setup and delivery avail-
able. Business established 1939.

Dar Furniture
517 S. Hamilton St.
High Point, NC 27260
(800) 631-3876
(910) 885-9193
Save 40 to 80% on showroom sam-
ples. Discounted prices available on
name brands, including: American
Drew, American of Martinsville,
Bassett, Councill Craftsman, Flexsteel,
Grand Manor, Hekman, Henry-
Link, Hickory White, Lexington,
Link-Taylor, Lyon-Shaw, Masterdesign,
Ridgeway, Singer, Stein World,
Universal, Webb, and Howard Miller
Clocks. Nationwide delivery and setup
available.

Davis Cabinet Co.
P.O. Box 60444
Nashville, TN 37206
$3 for catalog of reproduction
Victorian furniture.

The Decorator's Edge, Inc.
509 Randolph St.
Thomasville, NC 27360
(800) 289-5589
(910) 476-1047
Custom window treatments and
interiors. Save up to 75% off retail on
mini and micro blinds, 70% off on
wood blinds, 60% off on vertical

blinds, 20 to 40% off on fabrics, 20 to
40% off on wallpaper, 20 to 50% off
on furniture.

Decorum
235-237 Commercial St.
Portland, ME 04101
(207) 775-3346
Free information on their line of roll-
top desks, file cabinets, antique lamps,
bathroom and plumbing fixtures, and
hardware.

Deep River Trading Co.
2436 Willard Rd.
High Point, NC 27265
(919) 885-2436
Free information on 18th-century reproduction French, Victorian, and
country furniture. Early-American
dining and bedroom furniture, and
butcher blocks. Made from pine, oak,
walnut, cherry, and mahogany woods.
They also have available wicker pieces,
upholstery, and brass beds.

Derby Desk Co.
140 Tremont St.
Brighton, MA 02135
(617) 787-2707
Free information on antique desks.

Design-Kit
Main St.
Bloomingburg, NY 12921
Featuring kit-form furniture.

**Designer Home Furnishings of
Lexington, Inc.**
P.O. Box 1249
Lexington, NC 27293
(704) 798-1998
Free catalog of low-priced furniture,
accessories, crafts, and gifts for your
home, yard and office in country,
Colonial, Southwestern, and contemporary styles. Many unusual and hard-
to-find items. Satisfaction guaranteed.

Designer Secrets
Box 529
Fremont, NE 68025
$2 for catalog. Up to 50 percent
savings on window treatments,
wallpaper, accessories, fabrics,
bedspreads, and some furniture.

DMI Furniture Co.
Huntingburg, IN 47542
Send for information on their
discounted line of furniture.

Downtown Furniture Outlet
208 N. Elm St.
High Point, NC 27262
(800) 334-6796
(910) 882-2797
or
5626 Riverdale Drive
Jamestown, NC 27282-9113
(910) 454-9000
Vast savings on bedding and
furniture from many American
manufacturers. They offer
nationwide shipping.

Edgar B Furniture
P.O. Box 849
Clemmons, NC 27012
(800) 255-6589, (919) 766-7321
$25 for 308-page catalog. Up to 50
percent off retail prices on over 200
manufacturers of furniture and accessories. From traditional 18th-century
style to contemporary.

Clint Edwards, Cabinetmaker
5208 Brook Rd.
Richmond, VA 23227
(804) 266-1583
Send SASE for free information on
handmade reproduction furniture.

Fabian House
P.O. Box 86
Bowie, MD 20715

(301) 262-6606
$1 for catalog of Early-American
reproduction furniture, Windsor
chairs, tables, upholstered pieces, and
lighting.

Falcon Designs
91535 Deadwood Creek Rd.
Deadwood Creek, OR 97430
(503) 964-3191
$3 for catalog of heirloom-quality
cherry furniture.

Faucette's Furniture
2535 US Hwy. 70
Melbane, NC 27302
(919) 563-5271
Brand-name American manufactured
furniture at substantial discounts.
Brands include: American Drew,
Barcalounger, Bob Timberlake, Clay-
ton Marcus, Councill Craftsman,
Craftique, Hickory Chair, Hooker,
Lane, Leathercraft, Lexington, Link-
Taylor, Sedgefield, and Stiffel.
Business established 45 years. Shipping
available nationwide.

Alan Ferguson Associates
422 S. Main St.
P.O. Box 6222
High Point, NC 27262
(919) 889-3866
Featuring discounted unique, one-
of-a-kind furnishings for both residential and commercial interiors. Offer
ing upholstery, cabinetry, wood finishes
including faux or rich finishes, casegoods, fine art and sculpture, accessories, rugs and carpets, drapery and
upholstery fabrics, lamps, wallcoverings, and antiques. Delivery and
setup available nationwide.

Jeffrey Fliant,
Windsor Chairmaker
260 Gold Rd.

Reinholds, PA 17569
(215) 678-1828
$2 for brochure of reproduction
Windsor chairs.

Florida's Lifestyle
1805 NW 38th Ave.
Lauderhill, FL 33311
(800) 227-6060
Low-priced furniture, inside delivery,
and setup.

Frontier Furniture
260 Kelley Dr.
Bigfork, MT 59911
(406) 857-5194
$4 for catalog of log furniture, guard
rails, and accessories.

The Furniture Barn
11909 Hwy. 74 Bypass
Springdale, NC 28160
(704) 287-8785
Free information. Up to 50 percent
savings on 18th-century-styled furniture, imports, discontinued merchan
dise, mattresses, and accessories.

Furniture City Outlet
I-85 Business Loop
Thomasville, NC 27360
(910) 472-3677
Save up to 50% on brand name
furniture from over 200 American
manufacturers, including: American
Drew, Bassett, Benchcraft, Broyhill,
Dixie, England Corsair, Flexsteel,
Henry Link, Hooker, Lane, Lexington,
and Link Taylor. Nationwide shipping
and setup available.

Furniture Clearance Center
1107 Tate St.
High Point, NC 27260
(910) 882-1688
Wholesale prices on furniture.
Featuring showroom samples,
market samples, factory closeouts,

returned goods, duplicated orders,
and discontinued styles. Shipping
available nationwide.

Furniture Collections of Carolina
Rt. 8, P.O. Box 128
Hickory, NC 28602
(704) 294-3593
Free information on office and
interior furniture.

Furniture Company
322 Pine Mountain Rd.
Hudson, NC 28638
(704) 728-5001
Free information. Up to 40 to 60
percent savings on furniture and
accessories.

Furniture Connection of Carolina
(800) 869-5664
Call for information and quotes on
top lines of furniture.

Furniture Country U.S.A.
P.O. Box 946
Granite Falls, NC 28630
(800) 331-6724
Free information on furniture and
accessories.

Furniture Discount Resource
274 Eastchester Dr.
High Point, NC 27262
(800) 768-2535
Free information on furniture and
accessories.

Furniture From High Point
Special Orders:
1209 Greensboro Rd.
High Point, NC 27260
(800) 695-4814
(910) 454-4434 NC residents
Outlet:
1628 S. Main St.
High Point, NC 27260
(910) 454-8128

Specializing in the liquidation of name-brand market samples from the High Point furniture market. Brands include: Athens, Bassett, Bassett Mirror, Braxton Culler, Dale Tiffany Lamps, Emerson Leather, Hood, Lexington, Paul Robert Chair, Serta, Traditional France, Universal, and William Alan Upholstery. Shipping and setup available nationwide.

The Furniture Shoppe, Inc.
P.O. Box 703
Hudson, NC 28638
(704) 396-7850
Free brochures and ordering information. Discounted prices on national brands of solid-wood furniture.

Furniture Showcase
214 N. Main St.
High Point, NC 27261
(800) 234-1303
Free information. Up to 60 percent savings on furniture.

Furnitureland South, Inc.
Business I-85 at Riverdale Rd.
P.O. Box 1550
High Point, NC 27282
(910) 841-4328
Very large showroom (over 322,000 square feet) of discounted fine furniture and Oriental rugs in gallery settings. Including bedroom, dining room, leather, upholstery, office, outdoor, bedding, accessories, lamps, clocks, Oriental rugs, fine art. The following lines are represented: American Drew, Bernhardt, Broyhill, Century, Clayton Marcus, Cochrane, Drexel Heritage, Hickory-White, Lane, LaBarge, Leathercraft, Lexington, Pulaski, Stanley, Thomasville, and Virginia House. Nationwide shipping and setup.

G & G Furniture
10 E. Main St.
Thomasville, NC 27360
(800) 221-9778
Discounted prices on quality furniture. Bonded company.

Gibson Interiors
417 S. Wrenn
High Point, NC 27260
(800) 247-5460
(910) 889-4939
Over 150 styles and 300 colors of leather furniture featuring cost-plus pricing. They also carry a full line of lamps, mirrors, and all types of accessories. Leather brands include: Berkline, Emerson Leather, Glenncraft, Hickory International Design, Interline Italia, Leather Trend, and Yorkshire. They offer shipping nationwide.

Globe Furniture
1015 2nd St. NE, Ste. 205
Hickory, NC 28601
(800) 258-3273
Featuring discounted furniture prices and custom upholstery.

Gordon's Furniture Stores
214 N. Center St.
Statesville, NC 28677
(704) 873-4329
Mailing Address:
P.O. Drawer 1192
Statesville, NC 28687
Discount prices on brand-name furniture, including: La-Z-Boy, Gallery, Simmons, and Pennsylvania House.

Grand Furniture Marketing
(800) 528-1617
Line of glider rockers at discounted prices.

Great Meadows Joinery
P.O. Box 392

Wayland, MA 01778
(508) 358-4370
$4 for catalog of reproduction
Shaker and country-style furniture.

Grindstaff's Interiors
927 W. Main St.
Forest City, NC 28043
(704) 245-4263
Call or write for their free
brochure. Brands include: Baker,
Drexel-Heritage, Henredon, and
Pennsylvania House. Competitive
prices on over 200 lines of home
furnishings. Shipping available
nationwide.

**The Guild of Gulden
Cabinetmakers**
P.O. Box 66
Aspers, PA 17304
(717) 677-6146
$20 for catalog of reproduction
18th-century, handcarved and hand-
finished furniture.

Habersham Plantation
171 Collier Rd.
P.O. Box 1209
Toccoa, GA 30577
(800) 241-0716
$12 for catalog of contemporary
and reproduction 17th- and 18th-
century, country-styled furniture.

Habitat
947 Camino Santander
Sante Fe, NM 87501
Custom-made twig furniture.

Haig's Furniture
12605 E. Independence Blvd.
Mathews, NC 28105
(800) 737-8116
They offer excellent service and
prices on popular brands of
furniture from the U.S.A.

Hamilton Furniture
506 Live Oak St.
Beaufort, NC 28516
(800) 488-4720
They offer savings of up to 60
percent on nationally advertised
furniture. They have 48 years'
experience.

Harvest House Furniture
P.O. Box 1440
Denton, NC 27239
Free information. Up to 50 percent
savings off retail.

Heart-of-the-Wood Furniture
P.O. Box 3031
Plymouth, MA 02361
(508) 888-3552
$1 for brochure on reproduction
17th-century furniture.

Heath Craft Woodworks
Benton Harbor, MI 49022
Furniture available in kit form.

Heirloom Fine Furniture
1834 W. 5th St.
Montgomery, AL 36106
(800) 288-1513
$2 for catalog of reproduction
French and Victorian furniture.

Hickory Furniture Mart
2220 Hwy. 70 SE
Hickory, NC 28602
(704) 322-3510
Sixty-five galleries and factory outlets
with over 500 main manufacturers represented. Twelve acres of showrooms. Call for information and to be
directed to the desired gallery.

**Hickory-White Furniture
Factory Outlet**
1537 East Broad St.
Statesville, NC 28677

or
2629 Ramada Rd.
Burlington, NC 27215
(910) 229-0831
Factory owned outlet featuring
Hickory-White showroom samples,
market samples, discontinued living-
room, bedroom, and dining-room
furniture.

High Point Furniture Sales, Inc.
2000 Baker Rd.
High Point, NC 27260
(800) 334-1875
(910) 841-5664
Featuring fine furniture and
samples from 200 American
manufacturers including: American
Drew, Barcalounger, Bassett,
Benchcraft, Berkline, Brown-
Jordan, Broyhill, Clayton Marcus,
Flexsteel, Hickory White, Hooker,
Howard Miller, Kimball, Lane,
Lexington, Lloyd/Flanders, Lyon-
Shaw, Nathan Hale, Peoploungers,
Pulaski, Ridgeway Clocks, Riverside,
Sealy, Serta, Stratalounger, Tell City,
Thomasville, and Tropitone. Shipping
available nationwide. Full line of
interior furnishings represented.
Shipping available nationwide.

Hollingsworth American Country
P.O. Box 2592
Wilmington, NC 28402
(910) 251-0280
Free color brochure of fine-quality,
American country furniture. Bedroom,
pencil-post and sleigh beds, armoires,
entertainment and media centers, custom cabinets, etc. Priced from $695.

Holton Furniture Co.
805 Randolph St.
P.O. Box 280
Thomasville, NC 27360
(800) 334-3183
(910) 472-0400 NC residents

Featuring fine discounted furniture
from over 200 manufacturers. Brands
include: Action Recliners, American
Drew, Bassett, Benchcraft, Broyhill,
Classic Leather, Flexsteel, Hickory
White, Hooker, Howard Miller,
Kimball, Lane, Leathercraft,
Lexington, Lloyd/Flanders, Lyon-Shaw,
Meadowcraft, Nathan Hale, Peop-
loungers, Pulaski, Ridgeway Clocks,
Riverside, Sealy, Serta, Stanley,
Stanton Cooper, Tell City, Thomas-
ville, Virginia House Furniture, and
Woodmark. Shipping available nation-
wide.

Home Decorator Collection
2025 Concourse Dr.
St. Louis, MO 63146
(800) 245-2217
Free catalog of exterior accessories
of all types, furniture, clocks, lighting
fixtures, bathroom accessories, and
wicker.

Homeway Furniture Co.
P.O. Box 1548
Mt. Airy, NC 27030
(800) 334-9094
(919) 786-6151 NC residents
Free information. Up to 45 percent
savings on furniture.

Michael Houle Furniture
P.O. Box 1089
Marstons Mills, MA 02648
(508) 833-1399
$3 for catalog of reproduction
period furniture.

Martha M. House
1022 S. Decatur St.
Montgomery, AL 36104
(205) 264-3558
$3 for catalog. Reproduction
Victorian sofas, bedroom, dining,
tables and chairs.

House Dressing Furniture
3608 W. Wendover Ave.
Greensboro, NC 27407
(800) 322-5850
(910) 294-3900 NC residents
Free brochure. Discounted prices
on furniture with international
styling. Brands include: American
Drew, Barcalounger, Bassett, Bob
Timberlake, Childcraft, Chromecraft,
Classic Gallery, Flexsteel, Henry Link,
Hood, Hooker, Howard Miller, Kim-
ball, Lane, Lexington, Lyon-Shaw,
Madison Square, Nichols & Stone,
Pulaski, Riverside, Stanley, Stanton-
Cooper, Stratford, Stearns & Foster,
Tell City, Tropitone, and Virginia
House. Shipping available nationwide.
Full line of interior furnishings
represented. Special orders are
welcome. Shipping available nation-
wide.

House of Furnishings
Black Mountain, NC 28711
Offering discounted prices on
furniture.

Howerton Antique Reproductions
Clarksville, VA 23927
(804) 374-5715
$2 for catalog on handmade
reproduction furniture.

Hudson's Discount Furniture
P.O. Box 2547
Hickory, NC 28603
(704) 322-5717
Free information. Up to 50 percent
savings on furniture and accessories.

Hunt Galleries, Inc.
P.O. Box 2324. Dept. CL941
Hickory, NC 28603
(800) 248-3876, (704) 324-9934
$5 for 90-page color catalog. All types
of well-made transitional and contemporary upholstered furniture.

Hutchins Furniture
P.O. Box 1427
Kemersville, NC 27285
(800) 334-2408
Free information on furniture and
accessories.

Ian Ingersoll, Cabinetmakers
Main St.
West Cornwall, CT 06796
(800) 237-4926
$3 for brochure of reproduction
Shaker chairs and furniture.

IKEA, Inc.
P.O. Box 103016
Roswell, GA 30076-9860
(215) 834-0150
Check your yellow pages or call for
the nearest location and catalog. This
is a chain store offering Swedish-
styled, reasonably-priced furniture,
lighting, flooring, and accessories.
Satisfaction guaranteed.

Interior Furnishings, LTD.
P.O. Box 1644
Hickory, NC 28603
(704) 328-5683
$3 for brochure. Up to 45 percent
savings on furniture and accessories.

Interiors of High Point
1701-C N. Main St.
High Point, NC 27262
(800) 999-0520
(910) 887-0520 NC residents
They specialize in home offices and
feature discounted office, contract
furnishings, home furnishings, outdoor
furnishings, Oriental rugs, pictures,
accessories. Over 300 lines represented, including: Flexsteel, Hekman,
Hickory-Fry, Hooker, Lane, Lexington,
Tropitone, and Universal. They offer
nationwide shipping.

Irion Company Furniture Makers
44 N. Valley Rd.
Paoli, PA 19301
(215) 644-7516
Send SASE for free information on handmade, reproduction 18th-century furniture.

John-Michael Furniture
2113 Hickory Blvd.
Hudson, NC 28638
(800) 669-3801
Free information on furniture and accessories. Low prices on name-brand furniture.

Kagan's Furniture Galleries
Main Store:
1506 S. Main St.
High Point, NC 27260
(910) 889-8921
Atrium Location:
430 S. Main St.
High Point, NC 27260
(910) 885-8568
Exceptional prices on leading furniture brands, including: American Drew, American of Martinsville, Bassett, Bob Timberlake, Clayton Marcus, Flexsteel, Hooker, Lane, Lexington, Peoploungers, Stanley, and Universal. Shipping and setup available nationwide.

Kincaid Galleries
430 S. Main St.
High Point, NC 27260
(800) 883-1818
(910) 527-2570 NC residents
Free brochure of solid-wood furniture at discount prices. Large discounts on brand-name 18th-century Shaker and traditional furniture, wicker, recliners, bedding and accessories. Custom upholstery available. Brands include: Barcalounger, Custom Upholstery, Lane, Lloyd/Flanders, and Serta. Shipping available nationwide.

Knight Gallery
P.O. Box 1254
Lenoir, NC 28645
(800) 334-4721
Free information on furniture and accessories.

Thomas H. Kramer, Inc.
805 Depot St.
Commerce Park
Columbus, IN 47201
(812) 379-4097
$3 for catalog of period and country-styled furniture and accessories.

Lanier Furniture Company
P.O. Box 3576
Wilmington, NC 28406
(800) 453-1362
Call for information. Discounted prices on Shaker country furniture.

James Lea, Cabinetmaker
9 West St.
Rockport, ME 04856
(207) 236-3632
$5 for catalog of handmade, reproduction 17th- and 18th-century furniture.

Leather Interiors
P.O. Box 9305
Hickory, NC 28603
(800) 627-4526
Free information on classic and contemporary leather furniture.

LeFort Furniture
293 Winter St.
Hanover, MA 02339
(617) 826-9033
$6 for portfolio of furniture and accessories.

Liberty Green
P.O. Box 5035, Station 1
Wilmington, NC 28403
(800) 255-9704

$3 for catalog of handcrafted pine reproduction furniture.

Liberty Hall
P.O. Box 236
104 Fremont St.
Burgaw, NC 28425
(800) 255-9704
(919) 259-3493 NC residents
$3 for catalog of handcrafted pine reproductions of discounted classical and upholstered furniture. Satisfaction guaranteed.

Lincoln House Furniture
3105 Sulphur Springs Rd. NE
Hickory, NC 28601
$5 for catalog of leather furniture.

F. Lindsey
P.O. Box 551
Falls City, WA 58204
Send for information. Twig furniture manufacturer.

Lodgepole Furniture
Star Route, Box 15
Jackson, WY 83001
Featuring lodgepole-styled furniture.

Loftin-Black Furniture Co.
111 Sedgehill Dr.
Thomasville, NC 27360
(800) 334-7398
(919) 472-6117 NC residents
or
214 N. Main St.
High Point, NC 27262
(910) 883-4711
Send SASE for free information on over 300 major brands of furniture and accessories at discounted prices. Featuring bedroom, dining room, occasional, upholstered, bedding lamps, accessories, and pictures. Nationwide home delivery. Business established 1948.

Lounge Shoppe Furniture
2222-E Patterson St.
Greensboro, NC 27407
(800) 681-1982
Outlet prices for name-brand furniture. They will not be undersold. Brands include: Athens, Berkshire, Broyhill, Fashion House, Flexsteel, Henry Link, Hood, Lane, Leather Trend, Lexington, Link Taylor, Morgan Stewart, Stratolounger, Temple Stuart, Virginia House, and office furniture. Shipping available nationwide.

Mack & Rodel Cabinet Makers
Leighton Rd., RR1
P.O. Box 88
Pownal, ME 04069
(207) 688-4483
$4 for brochure of custom-made furniture.

Daniel Mack Rustic Furnishings
3280 Broadway
New York, NY 10027
(212) 926-3880
Send for information on rustic-styled furniture.

Magnolia Hall
726 Andover
Atlanta, GA 30327
(404) 237-9725
$3 for 80-page catalog of an assortment of furniture. Huge selection of sofas, beds, carved furniture, chairs, tables, lamps, clocks, mirrors, and desks.

Mahogany Craft
Park Alley Bldg.
16 E. Patrick St.
Frederick, MD 21701
(301) 663-4611
$5 for catalog of reproduction Chippendale bedroom, dining room furniture, and chairs.

Mallory's Furniture
P.O. Box 1150
Jacksonville, NC 28540
(919) 353-1828
Free brochure. Up to 60 percent
savings on furniture.

David & Susan Margonelli
RR1, P.O. Box 25852
Edgecomb, ME 04556
(207) 633-3326
$9 for portfolio of handmade
furniture.

Mathias & Coutler
1735 Pennsylvania Ave.
P.O. Box 2173
Hagerstown, MD 21742
(301) 791-2956
$3 for catalog of reproduction Early-
American and Colonial-styled
furniture.

Maynard House Antiques
11 Maynard St.
Westborough, MA 01581
(508) 366-2073
$2 for catalog of handmade Early-
American country sofas and wing-
styled chairs.

Mecklenburg Furniture Shops
520 Providence Rd.
Charlotte, NC 28207
(704) 333-5891
Free brochure on their line of
furniture and accessories.

Mid-America Furniture
P.O. Box 112
Hamburg, AR 71646
(800) 259-7897
Call for brochures and pricing.
Nationally advertised furniture at
unbeatable savings. 45 years'
experience.

Miya Shoji & Interiors, Inc.
109 W. 17th St.
New York, NY 10011
(212) 243-6774
Free brochure on custom Japanese
Shoji screens.

Montgomery Ward Direct
(800) 852-2711
Call for a free catalog featuring
discounted prices on bedding and bath
ensembles, bedspreads, accessories,
curtains, rugs, bedroom, living and
family room furniture.

E.T. Moore
3100 N. Hopkins Rd.
Richmond, VA 23224
(804) 231-1823
Free information on custom pine
furniture, mantels, columns, flooring,
moldings, paneling, and beams.

Thos. Moser Cabinetmakers
415 Cumberland Ave.
Portland, ME 04101
(207) 774-3791
$9 for catalog of handmade furniture.

Moultrie Manufacturing
P.O. Box Drawer 1179
Moultrie, GA 31776
(800) 841-8674
$3 for catalog of Southern-styled
reproduction garden and interior
furniture.

Murrow Furniture Galleries
P.O. Box 4337
Wilmington, NC 28406
(919) 799-4010
Free information. Up to 40 percent
savings on furniture.

Nite Furniture Company
611 S. Green St.
P.O. Box 249
Morganton, NC 28655

(704) 437-1491
Discounted prices on fine furniture,
including: Century, Classic Leather,
Drexel Heritage, Henredon, Hickory
Chair, Hickory White, Thomasville,
and Vanguard. They guarantee the
best service and prices. Business
established 1945.

**North Carolina Discount
Furniture Sales**
(919) 638-9164
Call for information. Mail-order sales
worldwide. They have available at
discount most major lines of furniture.

North Woods Chair Shop
237 Old Tilton Rd.
Canterbury, NH 93224
(603) 783-4595
$3 for catalog of handmade Shaker
furniture.

Northern Rustic Furniture
P.O. Box 11
Harrisville, MI 48740
$2 for brochure of unique willow-
and twig-inlay rustic furniture,
accessories, and frames.

Northwest Habitat Group
1421 N. Arbor
East Wenatchee, WA 98802
(509) 884-3708
Featuring furniture and decorative
items.

Oak-Wood Furniture Galleries, Inc.
3800 Comanche Rd.
Archdale, NC 27263
(910) 431-9126
Save up to 80% off retail on name-
brand American manufactured furniture, including upholstery, bedroom,
dining room, entertainment centers,
and accessories. Brands include:
American Drew, Bassett, Howard
Miller Clocks, Lexington, Pulaski,

Ridgeway, and Singer. Much of the
furniture is in stock. Offering nationwide shipping.

Olde Mill House Shoppe
105 Strasburg Pike
Lancaster, PA 17602
(717) 299-0678
$1 for catalog of braided rugs,
country-style handmade furniture,
linens, and bathroom accessories.

Old Wagon Factory
P.O. Box 1427
Clarksville, VA 23927
(804) 374-5787
$2 for catalog of Chippendale
furniture, Victorian railings, and
hardware.

Orleans Carpenters
P.O. Box 217
Orleans, MA 02653
(508) 255-2646
$3 for catalog of reproduction
Colonial and Shaker furniture.

Outer Banks Pine Products
P.O. Box 9003
Lester, PA 19113
They offer furniture in kit form.

Oxford Woodworks
80 Holsenbeck Dr.
Oxford, GA 30267
(404) 786-4159
$2 for catalog of unfinished furniture.

The Paper Place Interiors
606 Idol Dr.
P.O. Box 5985
High Point, NC 27262
(910) 869-8752
$3 for information. Discount prices
on 200 lines of name-brand wall
coverings, fabrics, blinds, shades,
and woven woods. Including Del

Mar window coverings, Dapha furniture, Marbro lamps, and Masland carpet.

Parkway Furniture Galleries
Hwy. 105 South
P.O. Box 2450
Boone, NC 28607
(704) 264-3993
Free information on their line of furniture and accessories.

Pennsylvania House Collectors' Gallery of High Point
P.O. Box 6437
1300 North Main St.
High Point, NC 27262
Mailing address:
P.O. Box 6437
High Point, NC 27262
(910) 887-3000
Clearance center with discounts of up to 50% on living-room, bedroom, dining-room, upholstery, leather furniture, bedding, rugs, entertainment units, lamps, and accessories. Pennsylvania House and other interior furnishings. They ship nationwide.

John & Debra Phillips
P.O. Box 402
Spring Hill, TN 37174
Send for information. Manufacturer of twig furniture.

Pier 1 Imports
Chain store all over the country.
(800) 447-4371
Call for the store nearest you. Featuring imported furniture and accessories from all over the world.

Plaza Furniture Gallery
241 Timberbrook Ln.
Hwy. 321
Granite Falls, NC 28630
(704) 396-8150
Free information on furniture and accessories.

Plexi-Craft Quality Products
514 W. 24th St.
New York, NY 10011
(800) 24-PLEXI
(212) 924-3244 NY residents
$2 for catalog. Up to 50 percent savings on Plexiglas and Lucite furniture, accessories, and fixtures.

Potcovers
101 W. 28th. St.
New York, NY 10001
Send for information. New twig furniture.

Priba Furniture Sales & Interiors
210 Stage Coach Trail
Greensboro, NC 27409
Mailing address:
P.O. Box 13295
Greensboro, NC 27415
Free information. Up to 45 percent savings on furniture, lighting, and accessories from over 250 major manufacturers. Brands include: Bernhardt, Broyhill, Chapman Classic Leather, Distinction Leather, Hickory Chair, Hekman, Hickory-White, Hooker, Karges, LaBarge, Lane, Leathercraft, Lenox Lighting, Lexington, Stanley, Stanton-Cooper, Statton, Thomasville, Vanguard, and Woodmark. Shipping available nationwide.

Quality Furniture Market of Lenoir, Inc.
2034 Hickory Blvd., S.W.
Lenoir, NC 28645
Send for information. Discounts on furniture, bedding, linens, accessories, and lamp shades.

Queen Anne Furniture, Inc.
10609 N. Main St.
Archdale, NC 27263

(800) 431-7209
(910) 431-7209 NC residents
Discount prices on name-brand
furniture, including: American Drew,
Bassett, Bob Timberlake, Broyhill,
Chatham County, County Seat,
Flexsteel, Henry Link, Kimball,
Hooker, Lexington, Link Taylor,
Pulaski, Richardson Bros., and Temple
Stuart. Nationwide in-home delivery
and setup.

Ralston Furniture Reproductions
P.O. Box 144
Copperstown, NY 13326
(607) 547-2675
$3.50 for brochure on reproduction
18th-century furniture.

Reflections
430 S. Main St.
High Point, NC 27260
(910) 885-5188
Offering elegant contemporary fur-
niture (including leather furniture).
Lines include Natuzzi, Lazar, Ekornes,
JRW Glass, Jaymar, and Design
Systems.

Rhoney Furniture
2401 Hwy. 70 SW
Hickory, NC 28602
Free information. Up to 50 percent
savings on classic and contemporary
furniture.

Dana Robes Wood Craftsmen
Lower Shaker Village
P.O. Box 707
Enfield, NH 03748
(603) 632-5385
$2 for catalog of reproduction Shaker
furniture.

Mario Rodriquez, Cabinetmaker
419 Manhattan Ave.
Brooklyn, NY 11222
$3.50 for brochure on handmade

reproduction furniture from the 18th
century.

Rose Furniture
916 Finch Ave.
High Point, NC 27263
(910) 886-6050
Clearance Store:
1813 S. Main St.
High Point, NC 27262
(910) 886-8525
Mailing address:
P.O. Box 1829
High Point, NC 27261
Three stories of discounted brand-
name furniture. Over 500 brands
represented, including: Bernhardt,
Councill Craftman, Hickory Chair,
Hickory-White, Hooker, LaBarge,
Lexington, Pennsylvania House,
Stanley, Stanton Cooper, Thomasville,
Virginia House, and Woodmark.
Business established 1925.

William James Roth
P.O. Box 355
Yarmouthport, MA 02675
(508) 362-9235
$4 for catalog of handmade
reproduction period furniture.

The Rounebush Co., Inc.
P.O. Box 348
Main St.
Star City, IN 46985
(800) 847-4947
Call for information about their
reproduction benches.

S.C.I.
102 E. Front St.
Burlington, NC 27215
(800) 252-8834
Discounted prices on Lexington,
Link-Taylor, Bob Timberlake, and
Key City furniture.

Sante Fe Country
1218 King St.
Alexandria, VA 22314
(800) 257-9577
Free catalog of Sante Fe country
accessories, gifts, and furniture.

Sanz International, Inc.
P.O. Box 1794
High Point, NC 27261
(919) 886-7630
Send SASE for free information on
wallcoverings, decorator fabrics,
carpeting, furniture, and lamps.

Sawtooth Valley Woodcrafts
4600 Ginzel
Boise, ID 83703
(208) 342-5265
Free brochure on handmade
reproduction log furniture.

Shaker Museum Gift Shop
Shaker Museum Rd.
Old Chatham, NY 12136
Send for information on their
collection of pre-assembled and kit-
form furniture.

Shaker Workshops
P.O. Box 1028
Concord, MA 01742
(617) 646-8985
$1 for 56-page color catalog of
Shaker furniture. Available in kit-
form or custom finished.

Shakercraft
P.O. Box 253
Hawesville, KY 43348
Handmade reproduction Shaker
furniture.

Shaw Furniture Galleries
Clearance Center
South Main at College Dr.
High Point, NC
(910) 889-4889

Retail Showroom
P.O. Box 576
Randleman, NC 27317
(919) 498-2628
Free information on 300 lines of
furniture and accessories with savings
of up to 40 percent off retail. Featuring order cancellations, showroom
samples, and factory closeouts. Brands
include: Bassett, Bernhardt, Broyhill,
Carsons, Classic Leather, Hickory
Chair, Hickory-White, and Thomasville. Nationwide delivery and setup.
Business established in 1940.

Shoji Workshop
21-10 31st Ave.
Astoria, NY 11106
(718) 274-9351
Send $.50 for information on their
Shoji screens.

Sobol House of Furnishings
Richardson Boulevard
Black Mountain, NC 28711
(704) 669-8031
Free information on brand-name 18th-
century-styled traditional or modern
furniture at savings from 40 to 50
percent off retail.

Solway Furniture, Inc.
120 Perimeter Park Dr.
Knoxville, TN 37922
(800) 422-8011
Free information on furniture and
accessories.

Southhampton Antiques
172 College Hwy., Rt. 10
Southhampton, MA 01073
(413) 527-1022
$25 for catalog of antique American
and Victorian furniture.

Southland Park Furniture Company
790 N. Main St.
High Point, NC 27261

(910) 886-7550
Substantial discounts on country
furniture, dinettes, and other
furnishings and accessories. Brands
include: American Table & Chair,
Bentwood, Caldwell Chair, Marlow,
and Stewart.

Spiegel Catalog
P.O. Box 6340
Chicago, IL 60680-6340
(800) 345-4500
$3 for catalog which includes a
range of interior products, furniture,
curtains, draperies, accessories, rugs,
lamps, etc. Many items discounted or
available discounted through subsequent sale catalogs. Satisfaction
guaranteed.

St. Charles Furniture
P.O. Box 2144
High Point, NC 27261
(800) 545-3287
Free information on furniture and
accessories. Discount prices on 150
lines of name-brand furniture. Their
brands include Broyhill, Hooker,
Kincaid, and Lexington.

Stephen Adams, Furniture Makers
Rt. 160, P.O. Box 130
Denmark, ME 04022
(207) 452-2444
$4 for catalog of furniture repro-
ductions of the 18th and 19th
centuries.

Strafford House
43 Van Sant Rd.
New Hope, PA 18938
(215) 598-0259
$2 for catalog of handmade and hand-
painted pine reproduction furniture.

Stratford Furniture Co.
666 N. Lake Shore Dr.
Chicago, IL 60611

Send for information on their
discounted line of furniture.

Straw Hill Chairs
RFD 1, Straw Hill
West Unity, NH 03743
(603) 542-4367
$2 for brochure of Windsor chairs.

Sturbridge Yankee Workshop
Blueberry Rd.
Westbrook, ME 04092
Send for catalog of traditional-
reproduction furniture and accessories.

Style Craft Interiors
P.O. Box 1725
Burlington, NC 27215
(800) 252-8834
Call for information. Discounted prices
on Bob Timberlake, Old Salem, and
Weekend Retreat accessories. Over 50
lines of furniture represented,
including Stanley and Lane.

Sutton-Council Furniture
P.O. Box 3288
Wilmington, NC 28406
(919) 799-1990
$5 for catalog of furniture and
accessories.

Suzanne's Chairs
509 Elm St.
Martins Ferry, OH 43935
(800) 225-4195
Featuring children's ladderbacks and
traditional rocking chairs with wicker
seats and hand-painted flower decorations.

Thomas Home Furnishings, Inc.
4346 Hickory Blvd.
Granite Falls, NC 28630
(704) 396-2147
Discounted prices on furniture for
living rooms, dining rooms, offices,
outdoors, bedding, and accessories.

(910) 886-7550
Substantial discounts on country
furniture, dinettes, and other
furnishings and accessories. Brands
include: American Table & Chair,
Bentwood, Caldwell Chair, Marlow,
and Stewart.

Spiegel Catalog
P.O. Box 6340
Chicago, IL 60680-6340
(800) 345-4500
$3 for catalog which includes a
range of interior products, furniture,
curtains, draperies, accessories, rugs,
lamps, etc. Many items discounted or
available discounted through subsequent sale catalogs. Satisfaction
guaranteed.

St. Charles Furniture
P.O. Box 2144
High Point, NC 27261
(800) 545-3287
Free information on furniture and
accessories. Discount prices on 150
lines of name-brand furniture. Their
brands include Broyhill, Hooker,
Kincaid, and Lexington.

Stephen Adams, Furniture Makers
Rt. 160, P.O. Box 130
Denmark, ME 04022
(207) 452-2444
$4 for catalog of furniture repro-
ductions of the 18th and 19th
centuries.

Strafford House
43 Van Sant Rd.
New Hope, PA 18938
(215) 598-0259
$2 for catalog of handmade and hand-
painted pine reproduction furniture.

Stratford Furniture Co.
666 N. Lake Shore Dr.
Chicago, IL 60611

Send for information on their
discounted line of furniture.

Straw Hill Chairs
RFD 1, Straw Hill
West Unity, NH 03743
(603) 542-4367
$2 for brochure of Windsor chairs.

Sturbridge Yankee Workshop
Blueberry Rd.
Westbrook, ME 04092
Send for catalog of traditional-
reproduction furniture and accessories.

Style Craft Interiors
P.O. Box 1725
Burlington, NC 27215
(800) 252-8834
Call for information. Discounted prices
on Bob Timberlake, Old Salem, and
Weekend Retreat accessories. Over 50
lines of furniture represented,
including Stanley and Lane.

Sutton-Council Furniture
P.O. Box 3288
Wilmington, NC 28406
(919) 799-1990
$5 for catalog of furniture and
accessories.

Suzanne's Chairs
509 Elm St.
Martins Ferry, OH 43935
(800) 225-4195
Featuring children's ladderbacks and
traditional rocking chairs with wicker
seats and hand-painted flower decorations.

Thomas Home Furnishings, Inc.
4346 Hickory Blvd.
Granite Falls, NC 28630
(704) 396-2147
Discounted prices on furniture for
living rooms, dining rooms, offices,
outdoors, bedding, and accessories.

Brands include: American Drew, Century, Clayton Marcus, Councill, Knob Creek, La-Z-Boy, Leathercraft, Lexington, Serta, Stanley, and Wellington Hall. Shipping available nationwide.

Thomasville Furniture Factory Outlet
401 E. Main St.
Thomasville, NC 27360
(910) 476-2211
Featuring factory close-outs, market samples, bedroom, dining room, upholstery, occasional and entertainment units.

Thornton's Furniture
400 McConnell Rd.
Greensboro, NC 27406
Send for information. Wholesale prices on furniture.

Tidewater Workshop
P.O. Box 456
Oceanville, NJ 08231
(800) 666-TIDE
Free brochure on factory-direct savings on cedar benches.

Chapin Townsend Furniture
P.O. Box 628
West Kingston, RI 02892
(401) 783-6614
$2 for brochure of custom, handmade reproduction 18th-century-period furniture.

R. Trammell & Sons Cabinetmaker
8519½ Chestnut Ave.
Historic Old Bowie, MD 20715
(301) 745-9347
$3 for catalog of cherry Shaker furniture with milk-paint finish.

Marion Travis
P.O. Box 292
Statesville, NC 28677

(704) 528-4424
(704) 872-5179 (after hours)
$1 for information on hardwood ladder-back chairs with handwoven-fiber rush seats.

Triad Furniture
3930 Hwy. 501
Myrtle Beach, SC 29577
(800) 323-8469
Call for information. Savings on North and South Carolinas' major furniture lines.

Triplett's Furniture Fashions
2084 Hickory Blvd.
Lenoir, NC 28645
(704) 728-8211
Free information on furniture and accessories.

Trott Furniture Company
P.O. Box 7
Richlands, NC 28574
(800) 682-0095
(919) 638-2121 NC residents
$5 for catalog of Oriental rugs, 18th-century mahogany, walnut and cherry furniture.

Turner-Tolson, Inc.
P.O. Drawer 1507
New Bern, NC 28560
(800) 334-6616
(919) 638-2121 NC residents
$2 for brochure on furniture and accessories.

Tysinger Furniture Gallery
P.O. Box 10339
Wilmington, NC 28406
(919) 799-137
Free information on furniture and accessories.

U.S.A. Furniture
547 Fulton St.
Brooklyn, NY 11201

(800) 846-7015
$5 for 162-page catalog of dinettes, bars, chairs, wood and occasional furniture, wall units, T.V. and stereo carts, daybeds, bunk beds, giftware, lamps, etc. Savings from 10 to 70 percent.

Utility Craft
2630 Eastchester Dr.
High Point, NC 27265
(910) 454-6153
Solid-wood 18th-century and traditional furniture and furnishings. Including bedroom, dining room, upholstery, leather, lamps, and accessories. Catalog sales available. Major brands include: American Drew, LaBarge, La-Z-Boy, Hekman, Lexington, Nichols & Stone, Pennsylvania Classics, Stanley, Stanton-Cooper, Statton, and Waterford. They ship and setup nationwide. Business established in 1949.

Valley Furniture
11843 E. Old Hwy. 64
Lexington, NC 27292-8912
(910) 472-3100
Specializing in discount-catalog sales of brand-name furniture manufacturers, including: American Drew, Bassett, Broyhill, Dixie, Flexsteel, Henry Link, Keller, Klaussner, Lexington, and Link Taylor.

Vance Furniture
325 S. Garrett St.
Henderson, NC 27536
(800) 438-3911
(919) 438-3911
Save 30 to 50% off retail on name brand furniture. Brands include: American Drew, American of Martinsville, Barcalounger, Berkline, Broyhill, Broyhill Premier, Bob Timberlake, Classic Leather, Clayton

Marcus, Jamestown Sterling, Leather Trend, Lexington, Link Taylor, Pulaski, Vaughn-Bassett, and Wicker by Henry Link. Shipping available nationwide.

Varner Furniture Sales
2605 Uharrie Rd.
High Point, NC 27263
(800) 334-3894
Free information. Save from 40 to 50 percent on furniture and accessories.

Village Furniture
P.O. Box 1148
Huntersville, NC 28078
$5 for catalog of Shaker furniture.

Walpole Woodworkers
767 East St.
Walpole, MA 02081
(508) 668-2800
$6 for catalog of handmade New England-styled cedar furniture.

Max Wardlow
RR 1
Fillmore, MO 64449
(816) 487-3385
$2 for catalog of Windsor and ladder-back chairs.

Warren's Interior Design & Furniture, Inc.
P.O. Box 33
Prospect Hill, NC 27314
(800) 743-9792
(910) 562-5198 NC residents
Up to 60% off retail on furniture from the following brands: Bassett, Clayton Marcus, Flexsteel, Henry-Link, Hooker, Leathercraft, Link-Taylor, Sealy Mattresses, White, and Howard Miller Clocks. Carpet brands include: Cabin Crafts, Masland, Philadelphia, and Sun. Fabric and wallpaper brands include: Greeff, Payne, and Schumacher. They also

have a large selection of pictures and accessories.

Wellington's Furniture
P.O. Box 2178
Boone, NC 28607
(800) 262-1049
Free information on their line of leather furniture.

The Wentworth Collection
P.O. Box 131
Wentworth, NH 03282
(603) 764-9395
$3 for information on their collection of reproduction period furniture.

White of Melbane
P.O. Box 367
Melbane, NC 27302
(919) 563-1217
Free brochure on 18th-century Early-American and English-styled furniture.

Whitson Furniture
Rt. 3, P.O. Box 157
Hwy. 64-70 W.
Newton, NC 28658
(704) 464-4596
Free information. Up to 50 percent savings on furniture.

Wicker Warehouse, Inc.
195 S. River St.
Hackensack, NJ 07601
(800) 274-8602
(201) 342-6709 NJ residents
Call for their catalog of wicker furniture and accessories.

Williams Country Furniture Store, Inc.
126 Church Lane
Cockeyville, MD 21030
(301) 666-5526
Call for their catalog of quality reproductions and furniture replicas

with hand-rubbed finishes. Quality and craftmanship since 1957. Satisfaction guaranteed.

Willsboro Wood Products
S. Ausable Dr.
Keeseville, NY 12996
(800) 342-3373
Free catalog of country-styled furniture, including Adirondack chairs and rocking chairs.

Windrift Furniture Gallery
145 Industrial Ave.
Greensboro, NC 27406
(919) 379-8895
Free information. Up to 40 percent savings on furniture and accessories.

Windsor Chairmakers
RR 2, P.O. Box 7
Lincolnville, ME 04849
(207) 789-5188
Free information on handmade Windsor furniture.

Windsor Furniture Galleries Clearance Center
607 Idol Drive
High Point, NC 27260
(910) 812-8000
Showroom
430 S. Main
In the Atrium
High Point, NC 27260
Exceptional savings of fine furniture, from traditional to contemporary, from many manufacturers, including: Century, Councill, John Widdicomb, Hickory White, Karges, Lexington, and Woodmark. Business established 40 years. Nationwide delivery and setup available.

Windsors by Bill Wallick
41 N. 7th St.
Wrightville, PA 17368
(717) 252-1240

$2 for brochure on handmade, reproduction Windsor chairs.

Windspire
P.O. Box 602
Fallston, MD 21047
Complete plans ($16.95 postage paid) for building rustic furniture from fallen trees and branches. Includes tables, chairs, beds, sofas, lamps, candlesticks, benches.

Melvin Wolf
61500 W. Cortland St.
Chicago, IL 60622
(312) 252-2800
Free information on brass furniture and beds.

Wood-Armfield Furniture Co.
460 S. Main St.
High Point, NC 27261
P.O. Box C
High Point, NC 27260
(910) 889-6522
Large showroom featuring fine furniture from 200 American manufacturers, including: Century, Classic Leather, Hickory-White, Knob Creek, LaBarge, Lexington, and Pennsylvania Classics. Full line of interior furnishings. Catalog sales and interior-design services. Ship and setup nationwide. Business established 1939.

Workshops of David T. Smith
3600 Shawhan Rd.
Morrow, OH 45152
(513) 932-2472
$5 for catalog featuring reproduction lamps, chandeliers, and furniture.

Yield House
P.O. Box 5000
North Conway, NH 03860
(800) 258-4720
Free information on country furniture,

curtains, accessories, and collectibles.

Young's Furniture and Rug Company
1706 N. Main St.
P.O. Box 5005
High Point, NC 27262
(910) 883-4111
Large discounts on major lines of fine furniture, including: Century, Councill, Hancock & Moore, Henredon, Hickory Chair, John Widdicomb, Karges, Lexington, Maitland-Smith, and Wright Table. Also includes upholstery, leather, accessories, and lamps. Business established 1946.

Zarbin & Associates
225 W. Hubbard, 5th Fl.
Chicago, IL 60610
Send for information. Furniture discounted up to 40 percent off retail.

Beds, Mattresses, and Box Springs

**Bedroom Furniture and
Mattress Discounters**
2020 S. Main St.
High Point, NC 27260
(910) 889-7378
Discounted prices on water mattresses
and bedroom furniture. Nationwide
delivery available.

**Bowen Town & Country
Furniture Co.**
4805 Shattalon Dr.
Winston-Salem, NC 27106
(910) 924-9311
or
1910 Mooney St.
Winston-Salem, NC 27103
(910) 765-1360
Discount prices on over 200 lines of
furniture, including: bedroom, dining
room, upholstery, occasional, accessories, office furniture, outdoor
furniture, wicker, leather, dinettes,
bedding, lamps, fine art. Available
brands include: Action, Broyhill,
Craftique, Hancock & Moore, Hekman, Henkel-Harris, Knob Creek,
Laine, Lane, Lexington, Sealy, Sligh,
Stanley, Statton, and Taylor-King.
Business established 1956. Nationwide
delivery and setup available.

Boyles Distinctive Furniture
727 N. Main St.
High Point, NC 27261
(910) 889-4147
or
616 Old Greensboro Rd.
High Point, NC 27260
(910) 884-8088
Featuring over 100 lines of fine
furniture discounted up to 50% off
retail. Including bedroom, dining
room, upholstered furniture, leather,
occasional, office, outdoor, bedding,
lamps, and accessories. Lines include:
Baker, Bernhardt, Century, Councill,
Drexel Heritage, Hancock & Moore,
Henkel-Harris, Henredon, Hickory,
Hickory Chair, Kingsdown, LaBarge,
Sherrill, Southwood, Statton, Sterns &
Foster, and Thomasville. Business
established 40 years.

Corner Hutch Furniture
(704) 873-1773
Highway 21 North
Statesville, NC 28677
(704) 873-1773
Discount prices on fine home
furnishings including the following
brands: American Drew, Barca-
lounger, Brown-Jordan, Century,
Chapman Lamps, Cochrane, Councill
Craftsman, Craftique, Distinctive
Leather, Emerson Leather, Haber-
sham Plantation, Henry-Link Wicker,
Hickory Chair, Hooker, Howard
Miller, Jamestown Sterling, LaBarge,
Lane, Lexington, Link-Taylor, Nathan
Hale, Pulaski, Sealy, Serta, Stanley,
Stiffel, Swan Brass Beds, Tropitone,
Wellington Hall, and Woodmark
Chairs. Shipping available
nationwide.

Dallas Furniture
215 N. Centennial St.
High Point, NC 27260
(910) 884-5759
Exceptional savings on quality
furniture, bedding, and accessories.
Brands include: American Drew,
Bassett, Broyhill, Flexsteel, Hooker,
Lane, Lexington, Lyon Shaw, Pulaski,
Singer, Spring Air Bedding, Strato-
lounger, Temple-Stuart, Universal, and
Howard Miller Clocks. Special orders
welcome. Nationwide setup and delivery available. Business established
1939.

Downtown Furniture Outlet
208 N. Elm St.
High Point, NC 27262
(800) 334-6796
(910) 882-2797
or
5626 Riverdale Drive
Jamestown, NC 27282-9113
(910) 454-9000
Vast savings on beds and furniture
from many American manufacturers.
They offer nationwide shipping.

Furniture From High Point
Special Orders:
1209 Greensboro Rd.
High Point, NC 27260
(800) 695-4814
(910) 454-4434 NC residents
Outlet:
1628 S. Main St.
High Point, NC 27260
(910) 454-8128
Specializing in the liquidation of
name-brand market samples from
the High Point furniture market.
Brands include: Athens, Bassett,
Bassett Mirror, Braxton Culler,
Dale Tiffany Lamps, Emerson
Leather, Hood, Lexington, Paul
Robert Chair, Serta, Traditional
France, Universal, and William
Alan Upholstery. Shipping and
setup available nationwide.

Furnitureland South, Inc.
Business I-85 at Riverdale Rd.
P.O. Box 1550
High Point, NC 27282
(910) 841-4328
Very large showroom (over 322,000
square feet) of discounted fine
furniture and Oriental rugs in gallery
settings. Including bedroom, dining
room, leather, upholstery, office,
outdoor, bedding, accessories, lamps,
clocks, Oriental rugs, fine art. The
following lines are represented:

American Drew, Bernhardt, Broyhill,
Century, Clayton Marcus, Cochrane,
Drexel Heritage, Hickory-White, Lane,
LaBarge, Leathercraft, Lexington,
Pulaski, Stanley, Thomasville, and
Virginia House. Nationwide shipping
and setup.

High Point Furniture Sales, Inc.
2000 Baker Rd.
High Point, NC 27260
(800) 334-1875
(910) 841-5664
Featuring fine furniture and samples
from 200 American manufacturers
including: American Drew, Barcalounger, Bassett, Benchcraft,
Berkline, Brown-Jordan, Broyhill,
Clayton Marcus, Flexsteel, Hickory
White, Hooker, Howard Miller,
Kimball, Lane, Lexington, Lloyd/
Flanders, Lyon-Shaw, Nathan
Hale, Peoploungers, Pulaski, Ridgeway
Clocks, Riverside, Sealy, Serta,
Stratalounger, Tell City, Thomasville,
and Tropitone. Shipping available
nationwide. Full line of interior
furnishings represented. Shipping
available nationwide.

Kincaid Galleries
430 S. Main St.
High Point, NC 27260
(800) 883-1818
(910) 527-2570 NC residents
Large discounts on brand-name
18th-century Shaker and traditional
furniture, wicker, recliners, bedding
and accessories. Custom upholstery
available. Brands include: Barcalounger, Custom Upholstery,
Lane, Lloyd/Flanders, and Serta.
Shipping available nationwide.

Loftin-Black Furniture Co.
111 Sedgehill Dr.
Thomasville, NC 27360
(800) 334-7398

(919) 472-6117 NC residents
or
214 N. Main St.
High Point, NC 27262
(910) 883-4711
Send SASE for free information on
over 300 major brands of furniture
and accessories at discounted prices.
Featuring bedroom, dining room,
occasional, upholstered, bedding,
lamps, accessories, and pictures.
Nationwide home delivery. Business
established 1948.

**Pennsylvania House Collectors'
Gallery of High Point**
P.O. Box 6437
1300 North Main St.
High Point, NC 27262
Mailing address:
P.O. Box 6437
High Point, NC 27262
(910) 887-3000
Clearance center with discounts of
up to 50% on living-room, bedroom,
dining-room, upholstery, leather furniture, bedding, rugs, entertainment
units, lamps, and accessories. Pennsylvania House and other interior
furnishings. They ship nationwide.

Thomas Home Furnishings, Inc.
4346 Hickory Blvd.
Granite Falls, NC 28630
(704) 396-2147
Discounted prices on furniture for
living rooms, dining rooms, offices,
outdoors, bedding, and accessories.
Brands include: American Drew,
Century, Clayton Marcus, Councill,
Knob Creek, La-Z-Boy, Leathercraft,
Lexington, Serta, Stanley, and
Wellington Hall. Shipping available
nationwide.

**Warren's Interior Design
& Furniture, Inc.**
P.O. Box 33

Prospect Hill, NC 27314
(800) 743-9792
(910) 562-5198 NC residents
Up to 60% off retail on furniture
from the following brands: Bassett,
Clayton Marcus, Flexsteel, Henry-
Link, Hooker, Leathercraft, Link-
Taylor, Sealy Mattresses, White,
and Howard Miller Clocks. Carpet
brands include: Cabin Crafts, Masland,
Philadelphia, and Sun. Fabric and
wallpaper brands include: Greeff,
Payne, and Schumacher. They also
have a large selection of pictures
and accessories.

Office Furniture, Supplies and Accessories

Alfax Wholesale Furniture
370 7th Ave., Ste. 1101
New York, NY 10001
(212) 947-9560
Free catalog offering office furniture, equipment, and office supplies.

Basil & Jones, Cabinetmakers
1150 17th St NW, Ste. 600
Washington, DC 20036
(202) 337-4369
Free brochure on custom wood or leather-accented desks in modern and period styling.

**Bowen Town & Country
Furniture Co.**
4805 Shattalon Dr.
Winston-Salem, NC 27106
(910) 924-9311
or
1910 Mooney St.
Winston-Salem, NC 27103
(910) 765-1360
Discount prices on over 200 lines of furniture, including: bedroom, dining room, upholstery, occasional, accessories, office furniture, outdoor furniture, wicker, leather, dinettes, bedding, lamps, fine art. Available brands include: Action, Broyhill, Craftique, Hancock & Moore, Hekman, Henkel-Harris, Knob Creek, Laine, Lane, Lexington, Sealy, Sligh, Stanley, Statton, and Taylor-King. Business established 1956. Nationwide delivery and setup available.

Boyles Distinctive Furniture
727 N. Main St.
High Point, NC 27261
(910) 889-4147
or
616 Old Greensboro Rd.
High Point, NC 27260
(910) 884-8088

Featuring over 100 lines of fine furniture discounted up to 50% off retail. Including bedroom, dining room, upholstered furniture, leather, occasional, office, outdoor, bedding, lamps, and accessories. Lines include: Baker, Bernhardt, Century, Councill, Drexel Heritage, Hancock & Moore, Henkel-Harris, Henredon, Hickory, Hickory Chair, Kingsdown, LaBarge, Sherrill, Southwood, Statton, Sterns & Foster, and Thomasville. Business established 40 years.

**Business & Institutional
Furniture Company**
611 N. Broadway
Milwaukee, WI 53202
(800) 558-8662, (414) 272-6080
Free catalog on office furniture and office equipment.

Derby Desk Company
140 Tremont St.
Brighton, MA 02135
(617) 787-2707
Free brochure of a line of antique roll-top and other styles of desks.

**Designer Home Furnishings
of Lexington, Inc.**
P.O. Box 1249
Lexington, NC 27293
(704) 798-1998
Free catalog of low-priced furniture, accessories, crafts and gifts for your home, yard, and office in country, Colonial, Southwestern, and contemporary styles. Many unusual and hard to-find items. Satisfaction guaranteed.

Frank Eastern Company
599 Broadway
New York, NY 10012
(212) 219-0007
Free catalog of office furniture,

equipment, and supplies.

Franz Stationery Company, Inc.
1601 Algonquin Rd.
Arlington Heights, IL 60005
Free catalog of office furniture,
equipment, and supplies.

Furniture Collections of Carolina
Rt. 8, P.O. Box 128
Hickory, NC 28602
(704) 294-3593
Free information on a collection of
office and interior furniture.

Furnitureland South, Inc.
Business I-85 at Riverdale Rd.
P.O. Box 1550
High Point, NC 27282
(910) 841-4328
Very large showroom (over 322,000
square feet) of discounted fine
furniture and Oriental rugs in gallery
settings. Including bedroom, dining
room, leather, upholstery, office,
outdoor, bedding, accessories, lamps,
clocks, Oriental rugs, fine art. The
following lines are represented:
American Drew, Bernhardt, Broyhill,
Century, Clayton Marcus, Cochrane,
Drexel Heritage, Hickory-White, Lane,
LaBarge, Leathercraft, Lexington,
Pulaski, Stanley, Thomasville, and
Virginia House. Nationwide
shipping and setup.

High Point Furniture Sales, Inc.
2000 Baker Rd.
High Point, NC 27260
(800) 334-1875
(910) 841-5664
Featuring fine furniture and
samples from 200 American
manufacturers including: American
Drew, Barcalounger, Bassett, Benchcraft, Berkline, Brown-Jordan,
Broyhill, Clayton Marcus, Flexsteel,

Hickory White, Hooker, Howard
Miller, Kimball, Lane, Lexington,
Lloyd/Flanders, Lyon-Shaw, Nathan
Hale, Peoploungers, Pulaski, Ridgeway
Clocks, Riverside, Sealy, Serta,
Stratalounger, Tell City, Thomasville,
and Tropitone. Shipping available
nationwide. Full line of interior
furnishings represented. Shipping
available nationwide.

Holton Furniture Co.
805 Randolph St.
Thomasville, NC 27360
(800) 334-3183
(910) 472-0400 NC residents
Featuring fine discounted furniture
from over 200 manufacturers. Brands
include: Action Recliners, American
Drew, Bassett, Benchcraft, Broyhill,
Classic Leather, Flexsteel, Hickory
White, Hooker, Howard Miller, Kim-
ball, Lane, Leathercraft, Lexington,
Lloyd/Flanders, Lyon-Shaw, Meadow-
craft, Nathan Hale, Peoploungers,
Pulaski, Ridgeway Clocks, Riverside,
Sealy, Serta, Stanley, Stanton Cooper,
Tell City, Thomasville, Virginia House
Furniture, and Woodmark. Shipping
available nationwide.

House Dressing Furniture
3608 W. Wendover Ave.
Greensboro, NC 27407
(800) 322-5850
(910) 294-3900 NC residents
Discounted prices on furniture with
international styling. Brands include:
American Drew, Barcalounger, Bas-
sett, Bob Timberlake, Childcraft,
Chromecraft, Classic Gallery, Flexsteel,
Henry Link, Hood, Hooker, Howard
Miller, Kimball, Lane, Lexington,
Lyon-Shaw, Madison Square, Nichols
& Stone, Pulaski, Riverside, Stanley,
Stanton-Cooper, Stratford, Stearns &
Foster, Tell City, Tropitone, and
Virginia House. Shipping available

nationwide. Full line of interior furnishings represented. Special orders are welcome. Shipping available nationwide.

Interiors of High Point
1701-C N. Main St.
High Point, NC 27262
(800) 999-0520
(910) 887-0520 NC residents
They specialize in home offices and feature discounted office, contract furnishings, home furnishings, outdoor furnishings, Oriental rugs, pictures, accessories. Over 300 lines represented, including: Flexsteel, Hekman, Hickory-Fry, Hooker, Lane, Lexington, Tropitone, and Universal. They offer nationwide shipping.

Jacob's Gardener Office Products & Furniture
5121 Buchanan St.
Hyattsville, MD 20781
(800) 638-0983
Free catalog of furniture and office supplies.

Kagan's Furniture Galleries
Main Store:
1506 S. Main St.
High Point, NC 27260
(910) 889-8921
Atrium Location:
430 S. Main St.
High Point, NC 27260
(910) 885-8568
Exceptional prices on leading furniture brands, including: American Drew, American of Martinsville, Bassett, Bob Timberlake, Clayton Marcus, Flexsteel, Hooker, Lane, Lexington, Peoploungers, Stanley, and Universal. Shipping and setup available nationwide.

Lounge Shoppe Furniture
2222-E Patterson St.

Greensboro, NC 27407
(800) 681-1982
Outlet prices for name-brand furniture. They will not be undersold. Brands include: Athens, Berkshire, Broyhill, Fashion House, Flexsteel, Henry Link, Hood, Lane, Leather Trend, Lexington, Link Taylor, Morgan Stewart, Stratolounger, Temple Stuart, Virginia House, and office furniture. Shipping available nationwide.

Thos. Moser Cabinetmakers
415 Cumberland Ave.
Portland, ME 04101
(207) 774-3791
$9 for catalog offering handmade furniture.

National Business Furniture, Inc.
222 E. Michigan St.
Milwaukee, WI 53202
(800) 558-1010
Free catalog of office furniture and supplies.

Office Depot
(800) 685-8800
Call for the nearest store near you. Low prices on office furniture, equipment, and office supplies.

Pyramid of Urbana
2107 N. High Cross Rd.
Urbana, IL 61801
(217) 328-3099
Free catalog of office furniture and supplies.

Queen Anne Furniture, Inc.
10609 N. Main St.
Archdale, NC 27263
(800) 431-7209
(910) 431-7209 NC residents
Discount prices on name-brand furniture, including: American Drew, Bassett, Bob Timberlake, Broyhill,

Chatham County, County Seat, Flex-steel, Henry Link, Kimball, Hooker, Lexington, Link Taylor, Pulaski, Richardson Bros., and Temple Stuart. Nationwide in-home delivery and setup.

Reliable Home Office
P.O. Box 804117
Chicago, IL 60607
(800) 326-6230
Free catalog offering furniture and supplies.

Scan Office Interiors
8406 Greenwood Pl.
Savage, MD 20763
(301) 953-2050
Free catalog of Scandinavian office furniture.

The Stand-Up Desk Company
5207 Baltimore Ave.
Bethsda, MD 20816
(301) 657-3630
Free brochure of collection of handmade desks.

Staples, Inc.
P.O. Box 160
Newton, MA 02195
Free catalog of office furniture, drafting equipment, supplies and office equipment.

Stuart-Townsend-Carr Furniture
P.O. Box 373
Limington, ME 04049
(800) 637-2344, (207) 793-4522
$4 for catalog of classic-styled office furniture.

Thomas Home Furnishings, Inc.
4346 Hickory Blvd.
Granite Falls, NC 28630
(704) 396-2147
Discounted prices on furniture for living rooms, dining rooms, offices,

outdoors, bedding, and accessories. Brands include: American Drew, Century, Clayton Marcus, Councill, Knob Creek, La-Z-Boy, Leathercraft, Lexington, Serta, Stanley, and Wellington Hall. Shipping available nationwide.

Warren's Interior Design & Furniture
P.O. Box 33
Prospect Hill, NC 27314
(800) 743-9792
(910) 562-5198 NC residents
Up to 60% off retail on furniture from the following brands: Bassett, Clayton Marcus, Flexsteel, Henry-Link, Hooker, Leathercraft, Link-Taylor, Sealy Mattresses, White, and Howard Miller Clocks. Carpet brands include: Cabin Crafts, Masland, Philadelphia, and Sun. Fabric and wallpaper brands include: Greeff, Payne, and Schumacher. They also have a large selection of pictures and accessories.

Woodshop
2966 Bay Rd.
Redwood City, CA 94063
(415) 365-1110
Free brochure of handmade reproduction desks and file cabinets.

Yield House
P.O. Box 5000
North Conway, NH 03860
(800) 258-4720
Free information on country curtains, accessories, collectibles, and furniture.

Antiques

The Antique Quilt Source
385 Springview Rd.
Carlisle, PA 17013
(717) 245-2054
$6 for current catalog and photos.
Unique selection of antique quilts
from Pennsylvania. Excellent condit-
ion. Satisfaction guaranteed.

**Century House Antiques
and Lamp Emporium**
46785 Rt. 18 West
Wellington, OH 44090
Send SASE for free information.
Custom shades and old shades,
supplies, and antique lamps.

Alan Ferguson Associates
422 S. Main St.
P.O. Box 6222
High Point, NC 27262
(919) 889-3866
Featuring discounted unique, one-
of-a-kind furnishings for both residential and commercial interiors.
Offering upholstery, cabinetry, wood
finishes including faux or rich finishes,
casegoods, fine art and sculpture,
accessories, rugs and carpets, drapery
and upholstery fabrics, lamps, wallcoverings, and antiques. Delivery
and setup available nationwide.

Kathryn's Collection
781 N. Main St.
High Point, NC 27260
Specializing in consignments, decorative accessories, antiques, and gifts
from showrooms, decorators and other
sellers.

Maynard House Antiques
11 Maynard St.
Westborough, MA 01581
(508) 366-2073
$2 for catalog of handmade Early-

American country sofas and wing-
styled chairs.

C. Neri Antiques
313 South St.
Philadelphia, PA 19147
(215) 923-6669
$5 for catalog of antique lighting
fixtures and accessories.

Rocky Mountain Quilts
2 Ocean Ave
Rockport, MA 01966
(800) 456-0892, (303) 464-7294
Quilts made from vintage fabrics,
antique and custom quilts, and quilt
restoration.

**Tysinger's Antiques (2 locations to
serve you)**
609 National Hwy.
Thomasville, NC 27361
(910) 883-4477
Direct importers of fine antiques
from England and France. Also
available at this location; decorative
accessories, art, and fine reproduction
furniture from the 18th and 19th
centuries, including: Baker, Kittinger,
Tomlinson, and John Widdicomb.
Business established 1959.

Randall Tysinger Collection
342 N. Wrenn Street
High Point, NC 27260
(910) 883-4477
Fine antiques only at this location.

**Thomas K. Woodard
American Antiques & Quilts**
835 Madison Ave.
New York, NY 10021
(212) 988-2906
$5 for catalog of Early-American area
rugs and runners.

Southhampton Antiques
172 College Hwy., Rt. 10
Southhampton, MA 01073
(413) 527-1022
$25 for catalog of antique
American and Victorian furniture.

Rattan and Wicker

Ashley Interiors
310 S. Elm St.
High Point, NC 27260
(910) 889-7333
Large collection of wicker and rattan furniture offered at factory direct prices. Also offering discontinued items and showroom samples. Custom orders are available. Nationwide shipping and setup.

Catherine Ann Furnishings
615 Loudonville Rd.
Latham, NY 12110
(518) 785-4175
They offer a catalog of outdoor all-weather wicker furniture.

Bowen Town & Country Furniture Co.
4805 Shattalon Dr.
Winston-Salem, NC 27106
(910) 924-9311
or
1910 Mooney St.
Winston-Salem, NC 27103
(910) 765-1360
Discount prices on over 200 lines of furniture, including: bedroom, dining room, upholstery, occasional, accessories, office furniture, outdoor furniture, wicker, leather, dinettes, bedding, lamps, fine art. Available brands include: Action, Broyhill, Craftique, Hancock & Moore, Hekman, Henkel-Harris, Knob Creek, Laine, Lane, Lexington, Sealy, Sligh, Stanley, Statton, and Taylor-King. Business established 1956. Nationwide delivery and setup available.

Deep River Trading Co.
2436 Willard Rd.
High Point, NC 27265
(919) 885-2436
Free information on 18th-century reproduction French, Victorian, and country furniture. Early-American dining and bedroom furniture, and butcher blocks. Made from pine, oak, walnut, cherry, and mahogany woods. They also have available wicker pieces, upholstery, and brass beds.

The Gazebo of New York
127 East 57th St., Dept. CL
New York, NY 10022
$6 for catalog of a large selection of quilts, duvet covers, dust ruffles, curtains, braided and rag rugs, pillows, antique and new wicker pieces, and other hand-crafted accessories.

High Point Furniture Sales, Inc.
2000 Baker Rd.
High Point, NC 27260
(800) 334-1875
(910) 841-5664
Featuring fine furniture and samples from 200 American manufacturers including: American Drew, Barcalounger, Bassett, Benchcraft, Berkline, Brown-Jordan, Broyhill, Clayton Marcus, Flexsteel, Hickory White, Hooker, Howard Miller, Kimball, Lane, Lexington, Lloyd/Flanders, Lyon-Shaw, Nathan Hale, Peoploungers, Pulaski, Ridgeway Clocks, Riverside, Sealy, Serta, Stratalounger, Tell City, Thomasville, and Tropitone. Shipping available nationwide. Full line of interior furnishings represented. Shipping available nationwide.

Holton Furniture Co.
805 Randolph St.
Thomasville, NC 27360
(800) 334-3183
(910) 472-0400 NC residents
Featuring fine discounted furniture

from over 200 manufacturers. Brands include: Action Recliners, American Drew, Bassett, Benchcraft, Broyhill, Classic Leather, Flexsteel, Hickory White, Hooker, Howard Miller, Kimball, Lane, Leathercraft, Lexington, Lloyd/Flanders, Lyon-Shaw, Meadow craft, Nathan Hale, Peoploungers, Pulaski, Ridgeway Clocks, Riverside, Sealy, Serta, Stanley, Stanton Cooper, Tell City, Thomasville, Virginia House Furniture, and Woodmark. Shipping available nationwide.

Home Decorator's Collection
2025 Concourse Dr.
St. Louis, MO 63146
(800) 245-2217
Free catalog of exterior accessories of all types, furniture, clocks, lighting fixtures, bathroom accessories, and wicker.

Kincaid Galleries
430 S. Main St.
High Point, NC 27260
(800) 883-1818
(910) 527-2570 NC residents
Large discounts on brand-name 18th-century Shaker and traditional furniture, wicker, recliners, bedding and accessories. Custom upholstery available. Brands include: Barcalounger, Custom Upholstery, Lane, Lloyd/Flanders, and Serta. Shipping available nationwide.

Suzanne's Chairs
509 Elm St.
Martins Ferry, OH 43935
(800) 225-4195
Featuring children's ladderbacks and traditional rocking chairs with wicker seats and hand-painted flower decorations.

Vance Furniture
325 S. Garrett St.
Henderson, NC 27536
(800) 438-3911
(919) 438-3911
Save 30 to 50% off retail on name brand furniture. Brands include: American Drew, American of Martinsville, Barcalounger, Berkline, Broyhill, Broyhill Premier, Bob Timberlake, Classic Leather, Clayton Marcus, Jamestown Sterling, Leather Trend, Lexington, Link Taylor, Pulaski, Vaughn-Bassett, and Wicker by Henry Link. Shipping available nationwide.

Wicker Gallery
8009 Glenwood Ave.
Raleigh, NC 27612
(919) 781-2215
Discount prices on all types of wicker and rattan furniture. Brands include: A & M Black, Bassett, Benchcraft, Braxton Culler, Capri Furniture, CEBU Imports, Clark Casual, Classic Rattan, Discovery Rattan, Dura Wicker, Ficks Reed, International Wicker, Lane, Lexington, Lloyd/Flanders, South Seas, Whitecraft. Nationwide delivery available.

Wicker Warehouse, Inc.
195 S. River St.
Hackensack, NJ 07601
(800) 274-8602
(201) 342-6709 NJ residents
Call for their catalog of wicker furniture and accessories.

Outdoor, Porch Furniture and Garden Accessories

Acorn Services Corp.
346 Still River Rd.
Bolton, MA 01740
(508) 779-5515
$2 for catalog of redwood garden
furniture, benches, and plant stands.

Adirondack Designs
350 Cypress St.
Fort Bragg, CA 95437
(800) 222-0343
Free catalog of redwood exterior
furniture at savings of 30 to 50
percent off retail.

Adirondack Store & Gallery
109 Saranac Ave.
Lake Placid, NY 12946
(518) 523-2646
Free catalog offering oak or maple
exterior furniture.

AK Exteriors
298 Leisure Ln.
Clint, TX 79836
$2 for catalog of cast-iron exterior
furniture.

Boyles Distinctive Furniture
727 N. Main St.
High Point, NC 27261
(910) 889-4147
or
616 Old Greensboro Rd.
High Point, NC 27260
(910) 884-8088
Featuring over 100 lines of fine
furniture discounted up to 50% off
retail. Including bedroom, dining
room, upholstered furniture, leather,
occasional, office, outdoor, bedding,
lamps, and accessories. Lines include:
Baker, Bernhardt, Century, Councill,
Drexel Heritage, Hancock & Moore,
Henkel-Harris, Henredon, Hickory,

Hickory Chair, Kingsdown, LaBarge,
Sherrill, Southwood, Statton, Sterns &
Foster, and Thomasville. Business
established 40 years.

Blake Industries
390 Pond St.
South Weymouth, MA 02190
Free information on exterior teak
furniture, cast-iron decorative poles,
fixtures and other exterior accessories.

Cambridge Square
5214 W. Market St.
P.O. Box 49005
Greensboro, NC 27419
(910) 852-4566
$4.00 for catalog offering unique and
elegant outdoor and indoor casual
furniture. Save up to 50% off retail on
name brands.

Catherine Ann Furnishings
615 Loudonville Rd.
Latham, NY 12110
(518) 785-4175
They offer a catalog of outdoor all-
weather wicker furniture.

Cedar Hill
2100 Northwestern Ave.
West Bend, WI 53095
(800) 443-5800
Line of red-cedar Adirondack
chairs and footrests.

Color-Tex Distributors
1102 Dorris Ave.
P.O. Box 7023
High Point, NC 27264
(800) 442-9049
(910) 886-3516
Call for information on wholesale
prices on name-brand furniture.
Brands include: American Drew,

Bassett, Cochrane, Flexsteel, Hekman, Hood, Hooker, King Hickory, Kingsdown, Lea, Lexington, Marlow, Nathan Hale, Universal, Virginia House, and Winston Patio. Offering superior service and value.

Conrad's Mail Order
475 Oberlin Ave., South
Lakewood, NJ 08701
(508) 772-0023
$2 for catalog featuring furniture, kitchenware, fabrics, accessories, lamps, floorcoverings, wallpaper, lighting fixtures, and lamps.

Dar Furniture
517 S. Hamilton St.
High Point, NC 27260
(800) 631-3876
(910) 885-9193
Save 40 to 80% on showroom samples. Discounted prices available on name brands, including: American Drew, American of Martinsville, Bassett, Councill Craftsman, Flexsteel, Grand Manor, Hekman, Henry-Link, Hickory White, Lexington, Link-Taylor, Lyon-Shaw, Masterdesign, Ridgeway, Singer, Stein World, Universal, Webb, and Howard Miller Clocks. Nationwide delivery and setup available.

Deep River Trading Co.
2436 Willard Rd.
High Point, NC 27265
(919) 885-2436
Free information on 18th-century reproduction French, Victorian, and country furniture. Early-American dining and bedroom furniture, butcher blocks. Pine, oak, walnut, cherry, and mahogany woods. They also have available wicker pieces, upholstery, and brass beds.

Furnitureland South, Inc.
Business I-85 at Riverdale Rd.
P.O. Box 1550
High Point, NC 27282
(910) 841-4328
Very large showroom (over 322,000 square feet) of discounted fine furniture and Oriental rugs in gallery settings. Including bedroom, dining room, leather, upholstery, office, outdoor, bedding, accessories, lamps, clocks, Oriental rugs, fine art. The following lines are represented: American Drew, Bernhardt, Broyhill, Century, Clayton Marcus, Cochrane, Drexel Heritage, Hickory-White, Lane, LaBarge, Leathercraft, Lexington, Pulaski, Stanley, Thomasville, and Virginia House. Nationwide shipping and setup.

The Gazebo of New York
127 East 57th St., Dept. CL
New York, NY 10022
$6 for catalog of selection of quilts, duvet covers, dust ruffles, curtains, braided and rag rugs, pillows, antique and new wicker pieces, and other hand-crafted accessories.

High Point Furniture Sales, Inc.
2000 Baker Rd.
High Point, NC 27260
(800) 334-1875
(910) 841-5664
Featuring fine furniture and samples from 200 American manufacturers including: American Drew, Barcalounger, Bassett, Benchcraft, Berkline, Brown-Jordan, Broyhill, Clayton Marcus, Flexsteel, Hickory White, Hooker, Howard Miller, Kimball, Lane, Lexington, Lloyd/Flanders, Lyon-Shaw, Nathan Hale, Peoploungers, Pulaski, Ridgeway Clocks, Riverside, Sealy, Serta, Stratalounger, Tell City, Thomasville, and Tropitone. Shipping available

nationwide. Full line of interior furnishings represented. Shipping available nationwide.

Holton Furniture Co.
805 Randolph St.
Thomasville, NC 27360
(800) 334-3183
(910) 472-0400 NC residents
Featuring fine discounted furniture from over 200 manufacturers. Brands include: Action Recliners, American Drew, Bassett, Benchcraft, Broyhill, Classic Leather, Flexsteel, Hickory White, Hooker, Howard Miller, Kimball, Lane, Leathercraft, Lexington, Lloyd/Flanders, Lyon-Shaw, Meadowcraft, Nathan Hale, Peoploungers, Pulaski, Ridgeway Clocks, Riverside, Sealy, Serta, Stanley, Stanton Cooper, Tell City, Thomasville, Virginia House Furniture, and Woodmark. Shipping available nationwide.

House Dressing Furniture
3608 W. Wendover Ave.
Greensboro, NC 27407
(800) 322-5850
(910) 294-3900 NC residents
Discounted prices on furniture with international styling. Brands include: American Drew, Barcalounger, Bassett, Bob Timberlake, Childcraft, Chromecraft, Classic Gallery, Flexsteel, Henry Link, Hood, Hooker, Howard Miller, Kimball, Lane, Lexington, Lyon-Shaw, Madison Square, Nichols & Stone, Pulaski, Riverside, Stanley, Stanton-Cooper, Stratford, Stearns & Foster, Tell City, Tropitone, and Virginia House. Shipping available nationwide. Full line of interior furnishings represented. Special orders are welcome. Shipping available nationwide.

Interiors of High Point
1701-C N. Main St.
High Point, NC 27262
(800) 999-0520
(910) 887-0520 NC residents
They specialize in home offices and feature discounted office, contract furnishings, home furnishings, outdoor furnishings, Oriental rugs, pictures, accessories. Over 300 lines represented, including: Flexsteel, Hekman, Hickory-Fry, Hooker, Lane, Lexington, Tropitone, and Universal. They offer nationwide shipping.

Larkspur Furniture Co.
274 Magnolia Ave.
Larkspur, CA 94939
(800) 959-8174
They offer a line of romantic outdoor seating.

Masterworks Willow Furniture
P.O. Box M
Marietta, GA 30061
(404) 423-9000
$2.50 for catalog of a line of willow furniture.

Moultrie Manufacturing
P.O. Box 1179
Moultrie, GA 31776
(800) 841-8674
$3 for catalog offering Southern-style, reproduction garden and interior furniture, and Colonial lanterns.

Northern Rustic Furniture
P.O. Box 11
Harrisville, MI 48740
$2 for brochure on unique willow and twig-inlay rustic furniture, accessories, and frames.

The Old Wagon Factory
P.O. Box 1427, Dept. CL14
Clarksville, VA 23927
(804) 374-5787

$2 for catalog offering Victorian porch
furniture and trim, planters and
benchs, home and garden accessories,
wooden storm-screen doors.

Stony Brae, Ltd.
(800) 282-8997
Call for information on their line of
garden accents.

Decorative Stencils

Adele Bishop
P.O. Box 3349
Kingston, NC 28502
(802) 362-3537
$3.50 for catalog of assorted styles of
stencils.

American Home Stencils, Inc.
10007 S. 76th St.
Franklin, WI 53132
$2.75 for catalog of 130 precut
country, romantic, floral, classic,
ribbon, children themes, and related
supplies.

Constance Carol
P.O. Box 899
Plymouth, MA 02360
(800) 343-5921
Free catalog of stencil designs and
curtains. Charge for swatches.

Great Tracers
3 N. Schoenbeck Rd.
Prospect Heights, IL 60070
$1 for brochure on lettering stencils.

Gail Grisi Stenciling, Inc.
P.O. Box 1263
Haddonfield, NJ 08033
(609) 354-1757
$2 for catalog of precut individual
stencils, kits, and supplies. Business
established in 1979. Customer satisfaction.

Imagination Station
1746 Broadway
Raynham, MA 02767
(508) 823-0851
$2.50 for catalog of stencil patterns.

The Itinerant Stenciller
11030 173rd Ave. SE
Renton, WA 98059
(206) 226-0306

$5 for catalog featuring elegant Jan
Dressler Stencils.

Jeannie Serpa Stencils
P.O. Box 672
Jamestown, RI 03835-0672
$3 for brochure of designer wall
stencils.

StenArt, Inc.
P.O. Box 114
Pitman, NJ 08071
$3 for catalog of stencil kits and
supplies.

Stencil House of New Hampshire
P.O. Box 109
Hooksett, NH 03306
(203) 635-1716
$2.50 for catalog of 175 designs of
precut and uncut stencils for formal
settings, family rooms, and children's
rooms. Includes authentic reproductions and stencil supplies.

The Stencil Shoppe
3634 Silverside Rd.
Wilmington, DE 19810
(800) 822-STEN
$3.95 for 44-page color catalog
featuring 775 stencil designs
ranging from $5.50 to $85.

Stencil World
1456 2nd Ave.
P.O. Box 175
New York, NY 10021
(212) 517-7164
$3.50 for catalog of pre-cut stencils
and supplies.

Tempo Stencils
P.O. Box 18611
Milwaukee, WI 53218
(414) 461-4640
Featuring pre-cut border patterns:

Victorian, Western, Oriental, and
other styles.

Yowler & Shepp Stencils
3529 Main St.
Conestoga, PA 17516
(717) 872-2820
$3 for catalog. Pattern styles include
ribbons, flowers, and vines.

Lighting and Lamps

18th-Century Tinware
1323 Twin Rd.
West Alexandria, OH 45381
(800) 950-5834
$2 for catalog of tin chandeliers,
lanterns, sconces, and candle molds.

A Brass Bed Shoppe
12421 Cedar Road
Cleveland Heights, OH 44106
(216) 229-4900
Free color catalog of large selection of
heirloom-quality, solid-brass and white
iron beds. Save 50 percent by buying
factory direct.

Alkco Lighting
11500 W. Melrose Ave.
P.O. Box 1389
Franklin Park, IL 60131
(708) 451-0700
Free information on lighting fixtures
and accessories.

Allied Lighting
3004 Columbia Ave.
Lancaster, PA 17603
(717) 392-5649
$1.50 for catalog representing over 40
manufacturers. Savings of up to 60
percent off retail on handcrafted
Early-American lamps, Tiffany lamps,
crystal chandeliers, lanterns, post
lamps, and accessories.

American Lighting
2531-108 Eastchester Dr.
High Point, NC 27265
(800) 741-0571
Free information about their line of
chandeliers.

Antique Hardware Store
9718 Easton Rd., Rt. 611
Kintersville, PA 18930
(800) 422-9982

$3 for catalog of reproduction tin and
wood chandeliers, interior and exterior
lamps, fixtures, sinks, toilets, and
hardware.

Arizona Mail Order
(800) 362-8415
$2 for Home Etc. catalog featuring
discounted prices on all types of
bedding and bath ensembles, bedspreads, quilts, linens, accessories,
curtains, and rugs.

Art Directions
6120 Delmar Blvd.
St Louis, MO 63112
(314) 863-1895
Reproduction, antique, and custom-
made lighting fixtures.

The Atrium
430 S. Main St.
High Point, NC 27260
(910) 882-5599
Furniture mall of 35 discount
galleries that represent over 650
furniture manufacturers. Offering
all types of furnishings, including:
accessories, Oriental rugs, lamps
and lighting. Call to be directed to
the gallery that carries specific lines
of furnishings. Featuring nationwide
delivery.

Authentic Designs
The Mill Rd.
West Rupert, VT 05776
(802) 394-7713
$3 for catalog offering handcrafted
reproductions of brass, tin, and copper
Early-American lighting fixtures and
chandeliers.

Baldwin Hardware Corp.
841 E. Wyomissing Blvd., P.O. Box
15048

Reading, PA 19612
$3 for catalog of lighting fixtures. $.75 for brochure featuring bathroom accessories, $.75 for brochure featuring door hardware, $.75 for brochure featuring decorative hardware.

Ball & Ball
463 W. Lincoln Hwy.
Exton, PA 19341
(215) 363-7330
$5 for catalog of reproduction chandeliers and lighting fixtures.

Barap Specialties
835 Bellows Ave.
Frankfort, MI 49635
(616) 352-9863
$1 for catalog of lamp parts, chair-caning supplies, turned-wood parts, etc.

Lester H. Berry & Company
P.O. Box 53377
Philadelphia, PA 19105
(215) 923-2603
They offer a line of reproduction brass chandeliers, sconces, table and desk lamps.

Blackwelder's
U.S. Hwy. 21 North
Stateville, NC 28677
(800) 438-0201, (704) 872-8922
$7.50 for catalog. Savings from 30 to 50 percent on office and home furniture, Oriental rugs, carpeting, lamps, etc.

Bowen Town & Country Furniture Co.
4805 Shattalon Dr.
Winston-Salem, NC 27106
(910) 924-9311
or
1910 Mooney St.
Winston-Salem, NC 27103

(910) 765-1360
Discount prices on over 200 lines of furniture, including: bedroom, dining room, upholstery, occasional, accessories, office furniture, outdoor furniture, wicker, leather, dinettes, bedding, lamps, fine art. Available brands include: Action, Broyhill, Craftique, Hancock & Moore, Hekman, Henkel-Harris, Knob Creek, Laine, Lane, Lexington, Sealy, Sligh, Stanley, Statton, and Taylor-King. Business established 1956. Nationwide delivery and setup available.

Boyles Distinctive Furniture
727 N. Main St.
High Point, NC 27261
(910) 889-4147
or
616 Old Greensboro Rd.
High Point, NC 27260
(910) 884-8088
Featuring over 100 lines of fine furniture discounted up to 50% off retail. Including bedroom, dining room, upholstered furniture, leather, occasional, office, outdoor, bedding, lamps, and accessories. Lines include: Baker, Bernhardt, Century, Councill, Drexel Heritage, Hancock & Moore, Henkel-Harris, Henredon, Hickory, Hickory Chair, Kingsdown, LaBarge, Sherrill, Southwood, Statton, Sterns & Foster, and Thomasville. Business established 40 years.

Brass Light Gallery
131 S. 1st St.
Milwaukee, WI 53204
(800) 243-9595
$3 for catalog of reproduction solid-brass chandeliers with glass shades.

Brasslight, Inc.
P.O. Box 695
Nyack, NY 10960

(914) 353-0567
$3 for catalog offering solid brass,
reproduction chandeliers, lamps,
and wall sconces.

Brass'n Bounty
68 Front St.
Marblehead, MA 01945
(627) 631-3864
Free information on available restored
antique chandeliers, floor lamps, and
sconces in electric, gas, or gas and
electric models.

Brubaker Metalcrafts
209 N. Franklin St.
P.O. Box 353
Eaton, OH 45320
(513) 456-1949
Free information on reproduction
Early-American tin and brass chandeliers, sconces, lanterns, and
other lighting fixtures.

Central Warehouse Furniture Outlet
2352 English Rd.
High Point, NC 27262
(910) 882-9511
Quality furniture offered at lower
prices. Including: living room,
bedroom, dining room, and kitchen
furniture. Market samples available at
substantial savings. Lamps, rugs, acces
sories, and pictures are also available.
Offering worldwide shipping.

**Century House Antiques
and Lamp Emporium**
46785 Rt. 18 West
Wellington, OH 44090
Send SASE for free information.
Custom shades and old shades,
supplies, and antique lamps.

City Lights
2226 Massachusetts Ave.
Cambridge, MA 02140
(617) 547-1490

$5 for catalog of restored antique
lighting fixtures and lamps.

Classic Illumination, Inc.
2743 9th St.
Berkeley, CA 94710
(510) 849-1842
$5 for catalog of lamps, and all types
of shades.

David L. Claggett, Artistry in Tin
P.O. Box 41
Weston, VT 05161
(802) 824-3194
$3 for catalog of reproduction tin
lighting.

Cohasset Colonials
271 Ship St.
Cohasset, MA 02025
(617) 383-0110
Reproduction Colonial furniture.
Available assembled, unfinished,
finished, or in kit form. They also
offer lighting fixtures, brass and
pewter accessories.

Conrad's Mail Order
475 Oberlin Ave., South
Lakewood, NJ 08701
(508) 772-0023
$2 for catalog offering furniture,
kitchenware, fabrics, accessories,
lamps, floorcoverings, wallpaper,
lighting fixtures, and lamps.

Copper Antiquities
P.O. Box 153
Cummaquid, MA 02637
$2 for brochure offering copper
Early American-styled lanterns.

Copper Lamps by Hutton
Rt. 940, P.O. Box 418
Pocono Pines, PA 18350
(717) 646-7778
Free information on all types of
reproduction Early-American

copper chandeliers and lamps.

A.J.P. Coppersmith & Company
20 Industrial Pkwy.
Woburn, MA 01801
(617) 932-3700
Colonial-reproduction chandeliers,
lanterns, sconces, cupolas, and weather
vanes made of copper, tin, and brass.

The Coppersmith
Rt. 20, P.O. Box 755
Sturbridge, MA 01566
$3 for catalog offering handcrafted
reproduction copper chandeliers,
sconces, and lanterns.

Corner Hutch Furniture
(704) 873-1773
Highway 21 North
Statesville, NC 28677
(704) 873-1773
Discount prices on fine home
furnishings including the following
brands: American Drew, Barca-
lounger, Brown-Jordan, Century,
Chapman Lamps, Cochrane, Councill
Craftsman, Craftique, Distinctive
Leather, Emerson Leather, Haber-
sham Plantation, Henry-Link Wicker,
Hickory Chair, Hooker, Howard
Miller, Jamestown Sterling, LaBarge,
Lane, Lexington, Link-Taylor, Nathan
Hale, Pulaski, Sealy, Serta, Stanley,
Stiffel, Swan Brass Beds, Tropitone,
Wellington Hall, and Woodmark
Chairs. Shipping available nationwide.

Country Curtains
Red Lion Inn
Stockbridge, MA 01262
Free 72-page catalog. Country-styled
curtains in cottons and cotton blends,
bedding, lamps and accessories.

COUNTRY STORE of Geneva, Inc.
28 James St.
Geneva, IL 60134

(708) 879-0098
$2 for catalog of country-styled tin
chandeliers, lamps, accessories, and
braided rugs.

Crawford's Old House Store
550 Elizabeth St.
Waukesha, WI 53186
(800) 556-7878
Free information on reproduction
Victorian and 1900's gas and electric
chandeliers and wall fixtures.

Decorum
235-237 Commercial St.
Portland, ME 04101
(207) 775-3346
Free information on line of roll-top
desks, file cabinets, antique lamps,
bathroom and plumbing fixtures, and
hardware.

Dibianco Lighting
8018 3rd Ave.
Brooklyn, NY 11209
(718) 238-7153
Free information on collection of
Italian contemporary lighting fixtures
in Murano glass.

Domestications
P.O. Box 40
Hanover, PA 17333-0040
(800) 746-2555
Free catalog of discounted bedroom
ensembles, curtains, accessories, and
lamps.

Elcanco, Ltd.
P.O. Box 682
Westford, MA 01886
(508) 392-0830
$1 for information on handcrafted
electric wax candles with flame-
shaped bulbs.

EMC Tiffany
45 Paris Rd.

New Hartford, NY 13413
(315) 724-2984
$3 for catalog featuring hand-
leaded Tiffany lamps.

Essex Forge
5 Old Dennison Rd.
Essex, CT 06426
(203) 767-1808
$2 for catalog of reproduction 18th-
century lighting fixtures.

European Classics
509 N. Virginia Ave.
Winter Park, FL 32789
(407) 628-8885
Free information on collection of
reproduction European lighting
fixtures.

Everything Ewenique
RR #1, P.O. Box 73
Mt. Pleasant Mills, PA 17853
(717) 539-2366
$4 for 52-page catalog offering
country lighting fixtures and
chandeliers.

Factory Paint Store
505 Pond St.
South Weymouth, MA 02190
(617) 331-1200
Free information on window
shades, wallpaper, paint and lighting
fixtures.

Fans
31567 U.S. 19
Palm Harbor, FL 34684
(800) 521-FANS
savings of up to 75 percent off manufacturer's prices. Also included are
other types of interior lighting.

Faucette's Furniture
2535 US Hwy. 70
Melbane, NC 27302
(919) 563-5271

Brand-name American manufactured
furniture at substantial discounts.
Brands include: American Drew,
Barcalounger, Bob Timberlake,
Clayton Marcus, Councill Craftsman,
Craftique, Hickory Chair, Hooker,
Lane, Leathercraft, Lexington, Link-
Taylor, Sedgefield, and Stiffel.
Business established 45 years. Shipping
available nationwide.

Alan Ferguson Associates
422 S. Main St.
P.O. Box 6222
High Point, NC 27262
(919) 889-3866
Featuring discounted unique, one-
of-a-kind furnishings for both residential and commercial interiors. Offering upholstery, cabinetry, wood
finishes including faux or rich finishes,
casegoods, fine art and sculpture,
accessories, rugs and carpets, drapery
and upholstery fabrics, lamps, wallcoverings, and antiques. Delivery and
setup available nationwide.

David H. Fletcher
Blue Mist Morgan Farm
68 Liberty St.
Haverhill, MA 01830
(508) 374-8783
$3 for catalog of copper lanterns and
weather vanes.

Frombruche
132 N. Main St.
Spring Valley, NY 10977
(800) 537-6319
$4 for catalog of custom brass, pewter,
brass and pewter combinations or
chrome lighting fixtures from the
1920s, Victorian, country French, and
English styles.

form + function
328 S. Guadalupe St.
Santa Fe, NM 87501

(505) 984-8226
$2 for color catalog of authentic Southwestern lighting. Included are table and floor lamps, and sconces.

Furniture From High Point
Special Orders:
1209 Greensboro Rd.
High Point, NC 27260
(800) 695-4814
(910) 454-4434 NC residents
Outlet:
1628 S. Main St.
High Point, NC 27260
(910) 454-8128
Specializing in the liquidation of name-brand market samples from the High Point furniture market. Brands include: Athens, Bassett, Bassett Mirror, Braxton Culler, Dale Tiffany Lamps, Emerson Leather, Hood, Lexington, Paul Robert Chair, Serta, Traditional France, Universal, and William Alan Upholstery. Shipping and setup available nationwide.

Furnitureland South, Inc.
Business I-85 at Riverdale Rd.
P.O. Box 1550
High Point, NC 27282
(910) 841-4328
Very large showroom (over 322,000 square feet) of discounted fine furniture and Oriental rugs in gallery settings. Including bedroom, dining room, leather, upholstery, office, outdoor, bedding, accessories, lamps, clocks, Oriental rugs, fine art. The following lines are represented: American Drew, Bernhardt, Broyhill, Century, Clayton Marcus, Cochrane, Drexel Heritage, Hickory-White, Lane, LaBarge, Leathercraft, Lexington, Pulaski, Stanley, Thomasville, and Virginia House. Nationwide shipping and setup.

Genie House
Red Lion Rd.
P.O. Box 2478
Vincentown, NJ 08088
$2 for catalog of handmade tin, copper, and brass reproduction 17th- and 18th-century lighting fixtures.

Georgia Lighting Supply Company, Inc.
530 14th St. NW
Atlanta, GA 30318
(404) 875-4754
Free catalog of American, Victorian, French, and English lighting fixtures.

Gibson Interiors
417 S. Wrenn
High Point, NC 27260
(800) 247-5460
(910) 889-4939
Over 150 styles and 300 colors of leather furniture featuring cost-plus pricing. They also carry a full line of lamps, mirrors, and all types of accessories. Leather brands include: Berkline, Emerson Leather, Glenncraft, Hickory International Design, Interline Italia, Leather Trend, and Yorkshire. They offer shipping nationwide.

Golden Valley Lighting
274 Eastchester Dr.
High Point, NC 27260
(800) 735-3377
Free information. $5 for 175-page color catalog. Up to 50 percent savings on lamps, fixtures, and accessories.

Hammerworks
6 Fremont St.
Worcester, MA 01603
(508) 755-3434
$3 for catalog offering copper Colonial reproductions of lanterns, chandeliers, and sconces.

Historic Housefitters
Dept. 1014
Farm to Market Rd.
Brewster, NY 10509
(914) 278-2427
$3 for 48-page catalog. The source-
book of 18th-century quality period
hardware and lighting. Handmade light
fixtures, brass, procelain and leaded
crystal door knobs, lever sets, etc.

Home Decorator's Collection
2025 Concourse Dr.
St. Louis, MO 63146
(800) 245-2217
(314) 993-1516 MO residents
Free catalog featuring lighting fixtures
and lamps. Included in the collection
are traditional and contemporary
styling, table and floor lamps, halogen
lamps, lamp shades, bathroom, ceiling,
wall and exterior fixtures and accessories.

Harry Horn, Inc.
622-624 South St.
Philadelphia, PA 19147
(215) 925-6600
$2 for catalog offering track- and
recessed-lighting fixtures.

Hubbardton Forge & Wood Corp.
P.O. Box 827
Castleton Corners
Castleton, VT 05735
(802) 468-3090
$3 for brochure of lamps, wrought-
iron and brass chandeliers, pan racks,
plant hangers, and bathroom
accessories.

IKEA, Inc.
P.O. Box 103016
Roswell, GA 30076-9860
(215) 834-0150
Check your yellow pages or call for
the nearest location and catalog. A
chain store offering Swedish-style,

reasonably-priced furniture, lighting
and accessories. Satisfaction
guaranteed.

Independence Forge
Rt.#1, P.O. Box 1-C
Whitakers, NC 27891
(800) 322-2702
(919) 437-2931
Call for information. Wrought-iron
lamps.

Juno Lighting, Inc.
P.O. Box 5065
Des Plaines, IL 60017
(708) 827-9880
Free information on available interior
and exterior lighting fixtures and
accessories.

Kemp & George
2515 E. 43rd St.
P.O. Box 182230
Chattanooga, TN 37422
(800) 562-1704
Free catalog of lighting fixtures,
bathroom fixtures and accessories,
and other home accessories.

King's Chandelier Company & Outlet
P.O. Box 667
Eden, NC 27288
(910) 623-6188
$3.50 for 100-page catalog offering
crystal chandeliers, candelabras and
sconces made from imported parts.
Considered the finest chandeliers
on the market. Prices less than wholesale. Save from 20 to 50 percent on
comparable-quality products.

KML Enterprises
R.R. 1, P.O. Box 234
Berne, IN 46711
$1 for catalog offering handmade
reproduction tin lanterns, chandeliers,
and sconces from the 18th century.

The Lamp Shop
4221 Garrett Rd.
Durham, NC
(919) 493-0661
Save 10 to 60% off retail on in-
stock lamps. Over 350 styles to
choose from. Framed prints are
20% off retail.

**Lamp Warehouse & New York
Ceiling Fan Center**
1073 39th St.
Brooklyn, NY 11219
(718) 436-8500
Send SASE for free information. Save
from 10 to 35 percent on lamps,
fixtures, and ceiling fans.

Leviton Manufacturing Company
59-25 Little Neck Pkwy
Little Neck, NY 11362
(718) 229-4040
Free information on available
interior and exterior lighting
fixtures, and accessories.

The Lighting Center
353 E. 58th St.
New York, NY 10022
Send for information. They offer a line
of lighting products.

Lightolier
100 Lighting Way
Secaucus, NJ 07096
(201) 864-3000
Free information on available interior
and exterior lighting fixtures, and
accessories.

The Linen Source
5401 Hangar Court
Tampa, FL 33631-3151
(800) 431-2620
Free catalog of discounted bedroom
ensembles, curtains, accessories, and
rugs. Satisfaction guaranteed. Business
established 56 years.

Luigi Crystal
7332 Frankford Ave.
Philadelphia, PA 19136
(215) 338-2978
$1 for catalog of line of crystal lamps,
chandeliers, and sconces.

Luma Lighting Industries, Inc.
410 W. Fletcher Ave.
Orange, CA 92665
(714) 282-1116
Free information on available interior
and exterior lighting fixtures and
accessories.

Lundberg Studios
P.O. Box C
Davenport, CA 95017
(408) 423-2532
$3 for catalog offering hand-blown,
antique-reproduction glass shades,
filter shades, and gas lights.

**Metropolitan Lighting
Fixture Company, Inc.**
315 E. 62nd St.
New York, NY 10021
(212) 838-2425
$5 for catalog of Art Deco, Art
Nouveau, period French, country
French, Colonial, and contemporary
lighting fixtures.

Montgomery Ward Direct
(800) 852-2711
Call for a free catalog featuring
discounted prices on bedding and
bath ensembles, bedspreads, accessories, curtains, rugs, bedroom, living
and family room furniture.

Gates Moore Lighting
2 River Rd.
Silvermine
Norwalk, CT 06850
(203) 847-3231
$2 for catalog featuring Early-
American copper chandeliers,

lanterns and sconces.

Moultrie Manufacturing
P.O. Box 1179
Moultrie, GA 31776
(800) 841-8674
$3 for catalog offering Southern-
styled Colonial reproduction lanterns,
garden, and interior furniture.

C. Neri Antiques
313 South St.
Philadelphia, PA 19147
(215) 923-6669
$5 for catalog of antique lighting
fixtures and accessories.

Newstamp Lighting Co.
227 Bay Rd.
North Easton, MA 02356
(508) 238-7071
$2 for catalog offering handmade
reproductions of Early-American
lamps, sconces, chandeliers and other
interior and exterior lighting fixtures.

Nowell's, Inc.
490 Gate 5 Rd.
P.O. Box 295
Sausalito, CA 94966
(415) 332-4933
$4 for catalog featuring antique
reproduction and restored chandeliers
and fixtures.

Packet Landing Iron Blacksmith
1022 Rt. 6A
West Barnstable, MA 02668
(617) 362-2697
Handmade reproduction wrought-iron
lamps and floor lamps, sconces, chandeliers and other lighting fixtures in
Early American, 18th-century, and
English styles.

Panet the Tin Man
195 Riverside Dr.

Troy, OH 45373
(513) 339-2315
$2 for catalog offering reproduction
copper, tin, and brass Colonial lamps
with an antique finish.

The Paper Place Interiors
606 Idol Dr.
P.O. Box 5985
High Point, NC 27262
(910) 869-8752
$3 for information. Discount prices
on 200 lines of name-brand wallcoverings, fabrics, blinds, shades, and
woven woods. Including Del Mar
window coverings, Dapha furniture,
Marbro lamps, and Masland carpet.

Hurley Patentee Lighting
R.D. 7, P.O. Box 98
Kingston, NY 12401
(914) 331-5414
$3 for catalog of line of handmade
reproduction Early-American lamps,
chandeliers, sconces, and lanterns.

**Pennsylvania House Collectors'
Gallery of High Point**
P.O. Box 6437
1300 North Main St.
High Point, NC 27262
Mailing address:
P.O. Box 6437
High Point, NC 27262
(910) 887-3000
Clearance center with discounts of up
to 50% on living-room, bedroom,
dining-room, upholstery, leather
furniture, bedding, rugs, entertainment
units, lamps, and accessories. Pennsylvania House and other interior
furnishings. They ship nationwide.

Period Lighting Fixtures
1 W. Main St.
Chester, CT 06412
(203) 526-3690

$3 for catalog featuring reproduction Early-American wood, tin, pewter, and copper chandeliers and lighting fixtures.

Priba Furniture Sales & Interiors
210 Stage Coach Trail
Greensboro, NC 27409
Mailing address:
P.O. Box 13295
Greensboro, NC 27415
Free information. Up to 45 percent savings on furniture, lighting, and accessories from over 250 major manufacturers. Brands include: Bernhardt, Broyhill, Chapman Classic Leather, Distinction Leather, Hickory Chair, Hekman, Hickory-White, Hooker, Karges, LaBarge, Lane, Leathercraft, Lenox Lighting, Lexington, Stanley, Stanton-Cooper, Statton, Thomasville, Vanguard, and Woodmark. Shipping available nationwide.

Progress Lighting
P.O. Box 12701
Philadelphia, PA 19134
(215) 289-1200
Free information on their line of interior and exterior lighting fixtures, and accessories.

Rejuvenation Lamp & Fixture Co.
901 N. Skidmore
Portland, OR 97217
(503) 249-0774
Reproduction brass turn-of-the-century lamps, chandeliers, and sconces.

The Renovator's Supply
Renovator's Old Mill
Millers Falls, MA 01349
(413) 659-2211
$3 for catalog offering reproduction lamps, ceiling fixtures, sconces, light fixtures, replacement-glass shades,

antique hardware, rugs, bathroom and plumbing fixtures, accessories, and curtains.

Roy Electric Company
1054 Coney Island Ave.
Brooklyn, NY 11230
(800) 366-3347
(718) 434-7002 NY residents
$6 for catalog of reproduction Art Deco, Victorian and 1900s-style chandeliers, fixtures and sconces.

St. Louis Antique Lighting Co., Inc.
801 N. Skinker
St. Louis, MO 63130
(314) 863-1414
$3 for catalog offering handmade reproduction brass lamps, ceiling fixtures, and sconces.

Salt Box, Inc.
3004 Columbia Ave.
Lancaster, PA 17603
(717) 392-5649
$1.25 for catalog offering brass, tin and copper reproduction Colonial chandeliers, lanterns, post lights, and foyer lights.

Sante Fe Lights, Inc.
Rt. 10, Box 88-Y
Sante Fe, NM 87501
(505) 471-0076
Showroom:
The Sante Fe Pottery
323 Guadalupe St.
Sante Fe, NM 87501
$2 for brochure of handcrafted stoneware, architectural lighting fixtures. Indoor and outdoor wall, ceiling and hanging lights, garden lights and chandeliers.

Shadowland Cove Lantern Company
P.O. Box 195
Cheshire, MA 01225

(413) 743-9020
$2 for catalog of available Colonial
reproduction chandeliers, post lights,
lanterns, and sconces.

Spiegel Catalog
P.O. Box 6340
Chicago, IL 60680-6340
(800) 345-4500
$3 for catalog offering a full range of
interior products, furniture, curtains,
draperies, accessories, rugs, lamps, etc.
Many items discounted or available
discounted through subsequent sale
catalogs. Satisfaction guaranteed.

Studio of Lights
2601 S. Main St.
High Point, NC 27260
(910) 882-6854
Discounted residential lighting fixtures.
Shipping available nationwide.

Studio Steel
P.O. Box 621
Wilton, CT 06897
$2 for catalog of handmade country
French and other styles of chandeliers.

Task Lighting Corp.
P.O. Box 1094
Kearney, NE 68848
(800) 445-6404
Free information on interior-lighting
fixtures and accessories.

The Tin Bin
20 Valley Rd.
Neffsville, PA 17601
(717) 569-6210
$2 for catalog of handmade country-
styled, electrified reproduction,
antiqued chandeliers made of brass or
copper.

Touch of Class
Order Dept.
1905 N. Van Buren St.

Huntingburg, IN 47542
(800) 457-7456
Free catalog. Bedroom and bathroom
ensembles, including bedspreads,
curtains, drapery, and fabric accessories, bathroom accessories, lamps,
and miscellaneous related accessories.

Utility Craft
2630 Eastchester Dr.
High Point, NC 27265
(910) 454-6153
Solid-wood 18th-century and tradition
al furniture and furnishings. Including
bedroom, dining room, upholstery,
leather, lamps, and accessories.
Catalog sales available. Major brands
include: American Drew, LaBarge,
La-Z-Boy, Hekman, Lexington,
Nichols & Stone, Pennsylvania
Classics, Stanley, Stanton-Cooper,
Statton, and Waterford. They ship
and setup nationwide. Business
established in 1949.

Victorian Lightcrafters, Inc.
251 S. Pennsylvania Ave.
P.O. Box 469
Centre Hall, PA 16828
(814) 364-9577
$3 for brochure of a line of
Victorian reproduction lighting
fixtures.

Village Lantern
P.O. Box 8
North Marshfield, MA 02059
$.50 for brochure on reproduction
Colonial chandeliers.

Washington Copper Works
49 South St.
Washington, CT 06793
(203) 868-7527
$3 for catalog offering handmade
copper lanterns and sconces.

Lt. Moses Willard, Inc.
1156 U.S. 50
Milford, OH 45150
(513) 831-8956
$3.50 for catalog of reproduction
Early-American chandeliers, lamps,
fixtures, sconces, candle holders, and
lanterns.

Workshops of David T. Smith
3600 Shawhan Rd.
Morrow, OH 45152
(513) 932-2472
$5 for catalog featuring reproduction
lamps, chandeliers, and furniture.

Young's Furniture and Rug Company
1706 N. Main St.
P.O. Box 5005
High Point, NC 27262
(910) 883-4111
Large discounts on major lines of fine
furniture, including: Century, Councill,
Hancock & Moore, Henredon, Hickory Chair, John Widdicomb, Karges,
Lexington, Maitland-Smith, and
Wright Table. Also includes upholstery, leather, accessories, and
lamps. Business established 1946.

Lamp Shades

American Deluxe Lighting
13543 Alondra Blvd.
Sante Fe Springs, CA 90670
(310) 802-8910
Free catalog of Handel-style hand-
blown glass and Tiffany-style shades.

American Lighting
2531-108 Eastchester Dr.
High Point, NC 27265
(800) 741-0571
Free information about their available
line of chandeliers.

Art Directions
6120 Delmar Blvd.
St Louis, MO 63112
(314) 863-1895
Reproduction, restored and custom-
made lighting fixtures.

Authentic Designs
The Mill Rd.
West Rupert, VT. 05776
(802) 394-7713
$3 for catalog offering handcrafted
reproductions of Early-American
lighting fixtures and chandeliers.

Ball & Ball
463 W. Lincoln Hwy.
Exton, PA 19341
(215) 363-7330
$5 for catalog featuring reproduction
chandeliers and lighting fixtures.

Brass Light Gallery
131 S. 1st St.
Milwaukee, WI 53204
(800) 243-9595
$3 for catalog of reproduction glass
shades and lamps.

Burdock Victorian Lamp Co.
1145 Industrial Ave.
San Diego, CA 92025

(619) 745-3275
Send SASE and $4 for brochure of
fringed polyester lamp shades and
lamp bases.

CDR Shade Company
P.O. Box 1030
Barrington, MA 01230
$2 for brochure on candle shades.

**Century House Antiques
and Lamp Emporium**
46785 Rt. 18 West
Wellington, OH 44090
Send SASE for free information on
custom shades, supplies, and antique
lamps.

Classic Illumination, Inc.
2743 9th St.
Berkeley, CA 94710
(510) 849-1842
$5 for catalog of lamp shades, and
all types of lamps.

Diversified Sales and Marketing
120 Old Mill Run
Ormond Beach, FL 32174
(800) 526-7586
Free information on available lamp
shades.

Einerlei
P.O. Box 679
Chassell, MI 49916
$1 for catalog of available lamp
shades.

Lampshades of Antique
P.O. Box 2
Medford, OR 97501
(503) 826-9737
$4 for catalog offering antique-
reproduction lampshades.

Lundberg Studios
P.O. Box C
Davenport, CA 95017
(408) 423-2532
$3 for catalog featuring hand-blown,
antique-reproduction, glass shades,
filter shades, and gas lights.

The Renovator's Supply
Renovator's Old Mill
Millers Falls, MA 01349
(413) 659-2211
$3 for catalog of reproduced antique
hardware, lighting, rugs, bathroom and
plumbing fixtures, accessories, and
curtains.

Shady Lady
418 E. 2nd St.
Loveland, CO 80537
(303) 669-1080
$3.50 for catalog of custom lamp
shades, or supplies to recover old
shades.

Unique Creations
28 Cherokee Dr.
Newark, DE 19713
(302) 737-8744
$.50 for catalog of their line of
sculptured lamp shades.

Clocks

Brentwood Manor Furnishings
316 Virginia Ave.
Clarksville, VA 23927
(800) 225-6105
Free brochure on fine-quality, name-brand furniture. Factory-direct prices on hundreds of brands of furniture, window treatments, draperies, accessories, clocks, and mirrors.

Dallas Furniture
215 N. Centennial St.
High Point, NC 27260
(910) 884-5759
Exceptional savings on quality furniture, bedding, and accessories. Brands include: American Drew, Bassett, Broyhill, Flexsteel, Hooker, Lane, Lexington, Lyon Shaw, Pulaski, Singer, Spring Air Bedding, Strato-lounger, Temple-Stuart, Universal, and Howard Miller Clocks. Special orders welcome. Nationwide setup and delivery available. Business established 1939.

Dar Furniture
517 S. Hamilton St.
High Point, NC 27260
(800) 631-3876
(910) 885-9193
Save 40 to 80% on showroom samples. Discounted prices available on name brands, including: American Drew, American of Martinsville, Bassett, Councill Craftsman, Flexsteel, Grand Manor, Hekman, Henry-Link, Hickory White, Lexington, Link-Taylor, Lyon-Shaw, Masterdesign, Ridgeway, Singer, Stein World, Universal, Webb, and Howard Miller Clocks. Nationwide delivery and setup available.

Emperor Clock Co.
Emperor Industrial Pk.

Fairhope, AL 36532
They have available a line of kit-form clocks.

Furnitureland South, Inc.
Business I-85 at Riverdale Rd.
P.O. Box 1550
High Point, NC 27282
(910) 841-4328
Very large showroom (over 322,000 square feet) of discounted fine furniture and Oriental rugs in gallery settings. Including bedroom, dining room, leather, upholstery, office, outdoor, bedding, accessories, lamps, clocks, Oriental rugs, fine art. The following lines are represented: American Drew, Bernhardt, Broyhill, Century, Clayton Marcus, Cochrane, Drexel Heritage, Hickory-White, Lane, LaBarge, Leathercraft, Lexington, Pulaski, Stanley, Thomasville, and Virginia House. Nationwide shipping and setup.

High Point Furniture Sales, Inc.
2000 Baker Rd.
High Point, NC 27260
(800) 334-1875
(910) 841-5664
Featuring fine furniture and samples from 200 American manufacturers including: American Drew, Barca-lounger, Bassett, Benchcraft, Berkline, Brown-Jordan, Broyhill, Clayton Marcus, Flexsteel, Hickory White, Hooker, Howard Miller, Kimball, Lane, Lexington, Lloyd/Flanders, Lyon-Shaw, Nathan Hale, Peop-loungers, Pulaski, Ridgeway Clocks, Riverside, Sealy, Serta, Strata-lounger, Tell City, Thomasville, and Tropitone. Shipping available nationwide. Full line of interior furnishings represented.

Holton Furniture Co.
805 Randolph St.
Thomasville, NC 27360
(800) 334-3183
(910) 472-0400 NC residents
Featuring fine discounted furniture from over 200 manufacturers. Brands include: Action Recliners, American Drew, Bassett, Benchcraft, Broyhill, Classic Leather, Flexsteel, Hickory White, Hooker, Howard Miller, Kimball, Lane, Leathercraft, Lexington, Lloyd/Flanders, Lyon-Shaw, Meadowcraft, Nathan Hale, Peoploungers, Pulaski, Ridgeway Clocks, Riverside, Sealy, Serta, Stanley, Stanton Cooper, Tell City, Thomasville, Virginia House Furniture, and Woodmark. Shipping available nationwide.

Home Decorator's Collection
2025 Concourse Dr.
St. Louis, MO 63146
(800) 245-2217
Free catalog of exterior accessories of all types, furniture, clocks, lighting fixtures, bathroom accessories, and wicker.

House Dressing Furniture
3608 W. Wendover Ave.
Greensboro, NC 27407
(800) 322-5850
(910) 294-3900 NC residents
Discounted prices on furniture with international styling. Brands include: American Drew, Barcalounger, Bassett, Bob Timberlake, Childcraft, Chromecraft, Classic Gallery, Flexsteel, Henry Link, Hood, Hooker, Howard Miller, Kimball, Lane, Lexington, Lyon-Shaw, Madison Square, Nichols & Stone, Pulaski, Riverside, Stanley, Stanton-Cooper, Stratford, Stearns & Foster, Tell City, Tropitone, and Virginia House. Shipping available nationwide. Full line of interior

furnishings represented. Special orders are welcome. Shipping available nationwide.

Magnolia Hall
726 Andover
Atlanta, GA 30327
(404) 237-9725
$3 for 80-page catalog of an assortment of furniture. Huge selection of sofas, beds, carved furniture, chairs, tables, lamps, clocks, mirrors, and desks.

Oak-Wood Furniture Galleries, Inc.
3800 Comanche Rd.
Archdale, NC 27263
(910) 431-9126
Save up to 80% off retail on name-brand American manufactured furniture, including upholstery, bedroom, dining room, entertainment centers, and accessories. Brands include: American Drew, Bassett, Howard Miller Clocks, Lexington, Pulaski, Ridgeway, and Singer. Much of the furniture is in stock. Offering nationwide shipping.

Old Town Clock Shop
3738 Reynolda Rd.
Winston Salem, NC 27106
(910) 924-8807
Large discounts on heirloom clocks. Brands include: Baldwin, Harrington House, Howard Miller, New England, Ridgeway, and Sligh. Nationwide delivery available.

Time Gallery
3121 Battleground Ave.
Greensboro, NC 27408
(910) 282-5132
Large clock showroom featuring discounted prices on all types of clocks, desks, curio cabinets, lamps, accent furniture, pictures, and accessories. Brands include: Ansonia,

Baldwin Clocks, Howard Miller, Ridgeway, Sligh Furniture, Superior Furniture, Wellington Hall. Lamps, accessories, pictures, globes and Baldwin Brass also available. Family owned and operated since 1984. Shipping available nationwide.

Warren's Interior Design & Furniture, Inc.
P.O. Box 33
Prospect Hill, NC 27314
(800) 743-9792
(910) 562-5198 NC residents
Up to 60% off retail on furniture from the following brands: Bassett, Clayton Marcus, Flexsteel, Henry-Link, Hooker, Leathercraft, Link-Taylor, Sealy Mattresses, White, and Howard Miller Clocks. Carpet brands include: Cabin Crafts, Masland, Philadelphia, and Sun. Fabric and wallpaper brands include: Greeff, Payne, and Schumacher. They also have a large selection of pictures and accessories.

Webster Imports
26201 Vermont Ave., Ste. 101B
Harbor City, CA 90710
$10 for catalog. Tremendous savings on heirloom-quality, handcarved cuckoo clocks. 300 models featured.

Fine Art and Framing

AJ Fine Arts
6208 Mill Lane
Brooklyn, NY 11234
(718) 531-7830
Competitive pricing on fine art. Will
try to beat competitors' prices.

Arron Bros, Art Marts
Look in your yellow pages for your
nearest location and phone number.
Low-priced chain store that has
posters, prints, and framing supplies.

Art Source
11548 West Trecker Way
Milwaukee, WI 53214
(800) 553-0081
Free 100-page wholesale catalog of
their best-selling art work.

Arts by Alexander
701 Greensboro Rd.
High Point, NC 27260
(910) 884-8062
Featuring unusual name-brand
contemporary, traditional, and
Oriental-styled furniture, accessories,
art and framing. Nationwide delivery
available. Business established 50 yrs.

Mitchell Beja, Inc.
1180 E 92nd St.
Brooklyn, NY 11236
(800) 847-4061
(718) 649-1617 NY residents
Savings on limited-edition graphics
and fine-art posters. They offer
best-selling, nationally-advertised art
posters from over 60 publishers.
Have been in business 16 years.

Bowen Town & Country
Furniture Co.
4805 Shattalon Dr.
Winston-Salem, NC 27106
(910) 924-9311

or
1910 Mooney St.
Winston-Salem, NC 27103
(910) 765-1360
Discount prices on over 200 lines of
furniture, including: bedroom, dining
room, upholstery, occasional, accessories, office furniture, outdoor
furniture, wicker, leather, dinettes,
bedding, lamps, fine art. Available
brands include: Action, Broyhill,
Craftique, Hancock & Moore, Hekman, Henkel-Harris, Knob Creek,
Laine, Lane, Lexington, Sealy, Sligh,
Stanley, Statton, and Taylor-King.
Business established 1956. Nationwide
delivery and setup available.

Exposures
41 S. Main St.
South Norwalk, CT 06854
(800) 222-4947
Free catalog of picture frames that
draw inspiration from Frank Lloyd
Wright, Charles Rennie Mackintosh,
Gustav Stickley, and other well-known
designers. Frames styles are based on
a range of periods.

Alan Ferguson Associates
422 S. Main St.
P.O. Box 6222
High Point, NC 27262
(919) 889-3866
Featuring discounted unique, one-
of-a-kind furnishings for both
residential and commercial
interiors. Offering upholstery,
cabinetry, wood finishes including faux
or rich finishes, casegoods, fine art and
sculpture, accessories, rugs and
carpets, drapery and upholstery
fabrics, lamps, wallcoverings, and
antiques. Delivery and setup
available nationwide.

Furnitureland South, Inc.
Business I-85 at Riverdale Rd.
P.O. Box 1550
High Point, NC 27282
(910) 841-4328
Very large showroom (over 322,000 square feet) of discounted fine furniture and Oriental rugs in gallery settings. Including bedroom, dining room, leather, upholstery, office, outdoor, bedding, accessories, lamps, clocks, Oriental rugs, fine art. The following lines are represented: American Drew, Bernhardt, Broyhill, Century, Clayton Marcus, Cochrane, Drexel Heritage, Hickory-White, Lane, LaBarge, Leathercraft, Lexington, Pulaski, Stanley, Thomasville, and Virginia House. Nationwide shipping.

Graphik Dimensions LTD.
2103 Brentwood St.
High Point, NC 27263
(910) 887-3500
Save up to 70% off retail on ready-made picture frames, moldings, supplies, mirrors, and prints.

J.B. Fine Arts, Inc.
420 Central Ave.
Cedarhurst, NY 11516
(800) 522-7872
(516) 569-5686 NY residents
Call for quotes and/or to receive a 12-page color brochure. They offer competitive prices on limited-edition serigraphs, lithographs, etchings, mixed media graphics, and bronze sculptures.

Peter Lane Fine Arts, Inc.
4433 Stirling Rd.
Ft. Lauderdale, FL 33314
(800) 998-LANE
(305) 583-7171 FL res.
Competitive prices on fine art.

Museum of Modern Art, New York
Mail-Order Dept.
P.O. Box 2534
West Chester, PA 19380
(212) 708-9888
$3 for catalog. Modern accessories for homes and offices.

Pacific Palm Fine Arts
77-594 Missouri Rd.
Palm Desert, CA
(619) 345-2656
They are always discovering new artists. Wholesale/retail art dealer offering discounted prices.

Pier 1 Imports
Chain store all over the country.
(800) 447-4371, call for the store nearest you. Imported furniture, accessories, frames, prints, and posters from all over the world.

Poster Originals, Ltd.
300 Hudson St.
New York, NY 10013
They offer a collection of posters.

Tysinger's Antiques (2 locations)
609 National Hwy.
Thomasville, NC 27361
(910) 883-4477
Direct importers of fine antiques from England and France. Also available at this location; decorative accessories, art, and fine reproduction furniture from the 18th and 19th centuries, including: Baker, Kittinger, Tomlinson, and John Widdicomb. Business established 1959.

Randall Tysinger Collection
342 N. Wrenn Street
High Point, NC 27260
(910) 883-4477
Fine antiques only at this location.

Accessories and Collectibles

Ad Lib
1401 W. Paces Ferry Rd.
Atlanta, GA 30327
(404) 266-2425
Free information on available
decorative accessories.

Amish Country Collection
Sunset Valley Rd., RD 5
New Castle, PA 16105
(800) 232-6474
Amish-style rugs, fabric accessories,
and other crafts. Hickory and oak
furniture in Amish style.

An Affair of the Hearth
P.O. Box 95174
Oklahoma City, OK 73143
(800) 755-5488
Free catalog of fireplace and related
accessories.

Architectural Sculpture Ltd.
242 Lafayette St.
New York, NY 10012
Architectural sculptures.

Arizona Mail Order
(800) 362-8415
$2 for Home Etc. catalog featuring
discounted prices on all types of
bedding and bath ensembles, bedspreads, quilts, linens, accessories,
curtains, and rugs.

Arts by Alexander
701 Greensboro Rd.
High Point, NC 27260
(910) 884-8062
Featuring unusual name-brand
contemporary, traditional, and
Oriental-styled furniture, accessories,
art and framing. Nationwide delivery
available. Business established 50
years.

Laura Ashley
1300 MacArthur Blvd.
Mahwah, NJ 07430
(800) 223-6917
$4 for catalog of English period repro-
ductions of window treatments, fabrics,
bedspreads, and other accessories.

The Atrium
430 S. Main St.
High Point, NC 27260
(910) 882-5599
Furniture mall of 35 discount
galleries that represent over 650
furniture manufacturers. Offering
all types of furnishings, including:
accessories, Oriental rugs, lamps
and lighting. Call to be directed to
the gallery that carries specific lines
of furnishings. Featuring nationwide
delivery.

Ballard Designs
1670 DeFoor Ave. NW
Atlanta, GA 30318
(404) 351-5099
$3 for catalog of furniture, fabric and
decorative cast accessories for interiors
and exteriors.

Barnes & Barnes Fine Furniture
190 Commerce Ave.
Southern Pines, NC 28387
(800) 334-8174
Send an SASE for free information.
Savings of up to 50 percent on
furniture, decorator fabrics, and
accessories.

Basketville, Inc.
Main St.
P.O. Box 710
Putney, VT 05364
(802) 387-5509
$2 for catalog of all types of woven
baskets.

C.H. Becksvoort
P.O. Box 12
New Gloucester, ME 04260
(207) 926-4608
$5 for catalog of handmade cherry
furniture and wood accessories in
traditional, Shaker or contemporary
styles.

Best Furniture Distributors
16 W. Main St.
P.O. Box 489
Thomasville, NC 27360
(800) 334-8000
Free information. Up to 40 percent
savings on furniture and wood accessories.

Best of Vermont
P.O. Box 775
Stowe, VT 05672
They have a collection of country
accessories.

Betsy's Place
323 Arch St.
Philadelphia, PA 19106
(215) 922-3536
$1 for brochure featuring brass repro-
ductions, sundials, and other
accessories.

The Bombay Co.
P.O. Box 161009
Fort Worth, TX 76161-1009
(800) 829-7789
Call for their free catalog and nearest
location. This is a chain store located
in larger malls. Reasonably-priced
traditional and Oriental furniture and
accessories.

Bonita Furniture Galleries
Rt. 5, P.O. Box 105
U.S. Hwy 321 North
Hickory, NC 28601
(704) 396-3178
Free information on their line of

furniture and accessories.

**Bowen Town & Country
Furniture Co.**
4805 Shattalon Dr.
Winston-Salem, NC 27106
(910) 924-9311
or
1910 Mooney St.
Winston-Salem, NC 27103
(910) 765-1360
Discount prices on over 200 lines of
furniture, including: bedroom, dining
room, upholstery, occasional, accessories, office furniture, outdoor
furniture, wicker, leather, dinettes,
bedding, lamps, fine art. Available
brands include: Action, Broyhill,
Craftique, Hancock & Moore, Hekman, Henkel-Harris, Knob Creek,
Laine, Lane, Lexington, Sealy, Sligh,
Stanley, Statton, and Taylor-King.
Business established 1956. Nationwide
delivery and setup.

Boyles Distinctive Furniture
727 N. Main St.
High Point, NC 27261
(910) 889-4147
or
616 Old Greensboro Rd.
High Point, NC 27260
(910) 884-8088
Featuring over 100 lines of fine
furniture discounted up to 50% off
retail. Including bedroom, dining
room, upholstered furniture, leather,
occasional, office, outdoor, bedding,
lamps, and accessories. Lines include:
Baker, Bernhardt, Century, Councill,
Drexel Heritage, Hancock & Moore,
Henkel-Harris, Henredon, Hickory,
Hickory Chair, Kingsdown, LaBarge,
Sherrill, Southwood, Statton, Sterns
& Foster, and Thomasville. Business
established 40 years.

Brentwood Manor Furnishings
316 Virginia Ave.
Clarksville, VA 23927
(800) 225-6105
Free brochure of fine-quality, name-brand furniture. Factory-direct prices on hundreds of brands of furniture, window treatments, draperies, accessories, including clocks and mirrors.

Carolina Furniture Gallery
Rt.1, P.O. Box 37A
Thomasville, NC 27360
(919) 475-1309
Free information on furniture and accessories.

Casual Living
5401 Hangar Ct.
P.O. Box 31273
Tampa, FL 33631-3273
(800) 843-1881
Call for catalog. Range of gifts and home accessories. Business established in 1953.

Central Warehouse Furniture Outlet
2352 English Rd.
High Point, NC 27262
(910) 882-9511
Quality furniture offered at lower prices. Including: living room, bedroom, dining room, and kitchen furniture. Market samples available at substantial savings. Lamps, rugs, accessories, and pictures are also available. Offering worldwide shipping.

Coffey Furniture Galleries
P.O. Box 141
Granite Falls, NC 28630
(704) 396-2900
Free information on furniture and accessories.

Cohasset Colonials
271 Ship St.

Cohasset, MA 02025
(617) 383-0110
Reproduction Colonial furniture. Available assembled, unfinished, finished, or in kit form. They also have a line of lighting fixtures, brass and pewter accessories.

Conrad's Mail Order
475 Oberlin Ave., South
Lakewood, NJ 08701
(508) 772-0023
$2 for catalog offering furniture, kitchenware, fabrics, accessories, lamps, floorcoverings, wallpaper, lighting fixtures and lamps.

Country Curtains
Red Lion Inn
Stockbridge, MA 01262
Free 72-page catalog of country-styled curtains in cottons and cotton blends, bedding, lamps, and accessories.

The Country House
805 E. Main St.
Salisbury, MD 21801
(410) 749-1959
$2 for catalog of extensive selection of Colonial home furnishings.

Country Manor
Mail-Order Dept.
Rt. 211
P.O. Box 520
Sperryville, VA 22740
(800) 344-8354
$2 for catalog of kitchen accessories and utensils, rugs and carpets.

The Country Mouse
P.O. Box 176
Harwinton, CT 06791
(203) 485-1419
Free catalog of antique-reproduction, decorative accessories for interiors and exteriors.

Country Sampler
P.O. Box 228
St. Charles, IL 60174
(708) 377-8000 for subscriptions.
This is a magazine available at bookstores and grocery stores for $4 per
copy that is <u>filled</u> with decorative
country accessories, folk art, and reproductions from a nationwide network of artistans and crafters who ship
directly to you.

COUNTRY STORE of Geneva, Inc.
28 James St.
Geneva, IL 60134
(708) 879-0098
$2 for catalog of country-styled tin
chandeliers, lamps, accessories, and
braided rugs.

Crafts Manufacturing Company
72 Massachusetts Ave.
Lundenburg, MA 01462
(508) 342-1717
$.50 for catalog of handmade Early-
American tinware, candleholders,
lamps, sconces, and trays.

Dallas Furniture
215 N. Centennial St.
High Point, NC 27260
(910) 884-5759
Exceptional savings on quality
furniture, bedding, and accessories.
Brands include: American Drew,
Bassett, Broyhill, Flexsteel, Hooker,
Lane, Lexington, Lyon Shaw, Pulaski,
Singer, Spring Air Bedding, Strato-
lounger, Temple-Stuart, Universal, and
Howard Miller Clocks. Special orders
welcome. Nationwide setup and
delivery available. Business established
1939.

Domestications
P.O. Box 40
Hanover, PA 17333-0040
(800) 746-2555

Free catalog of discounted bedroom
ensembles, curtains, accessories, and
lamps.

Edgar B. Furniture
P.O. Box 849
Clemmons, NC 27012
(800) 255-6589
$15 for 132-page catalog. Up to 50
percent off retail prices on over 130
manufacturers on furniture and acces
sories.

Farmer's Daughter
P.O. Box 1071
Nags Head, NC 27959
(800) 423-2196
$2 for catalog offering country-style
accessories, candles, potpourri, and
candle lamps.

Alan Ferguson Associates
422 S. Main St.
P.O. Box 6222
High Point, NC 27262
(919) 889-3866
Featuring discounted unique, one-
of-a-kind furnishings for both residential and commercial interiors.
Offering upholstery, cabinetry, wood
finishes including faux or rich finishes,
casegoods, fine art and sculpture,
accessories, rugs and carpets, drapery
and upholstery fabrics, lamps, wallcoverings, and antiques. Delivery and
setup available nationwide.

Flowers For You
P.O. Box 935
Eagle, Idaho 83616
$3 for catalog of dried roses and
flowers.

Fortunes
150 Chestnut St.
San Francisco, CA 94111-1004
(800) 331-2300
Free catalog offering a range of

accessories.

Frontier Furniture
260 Kelley Dr.
Bigfork, MT 59911
(406) 5194
$4 for catalog of log furniture, guard
rails, and accessories.

The Furniture Barn
11909 Hwy. 74 Bypass
Springdale, NC 28160
Free information. Up to 50 percent
savings on furniture, mattresses, and
accessories.

Furniture Company
322 Pine Mountain Rd.
Hudson, NC 28638
(704) 728-5001
Free information. Up to 40 to 60
percent savings on furniture and
accessories.

Furniture Country U.S.A.
P.O. Box 946
Granite Falls, NC 28630
(800) 331-6724
Free information on furniture and
accessories.

Furniture Discount Resource
274 Eastchester Dr.
High Point, NC 27262
(800) 768-2535
Free information on furniture and
accessories.

Furnitureland South, Inc.
Business I-85 at Riverdale Rd.
P.O. Box 1550
High Point, NC 27282
(910) 841-4328
Very large showroom (over 322,000
square feet) of discounted fine
furniture and Oriental rugs in gallery
settings. Including bedroom, dining
room, leather, upholstery, office,

outdoor, bedding, accessories, lamps,
clocks, Oriental rugs, fine art. The
following lines are represented:
American Drew, Bernhardt, Broyhill,
Century, Clayton Marcus, Cochrane,
Drexel Heritage, Hickory-White, Lane,
LaBarge, Leathercraft, Lexington,
Pulaski, Stanley, Thomasville, and
Virginia House. Nationwide
shipping and setup.

G & G Furniture
10 E. Main St.
(800) 221-9778
Thomasville, NC 27360
(800) 221-9778
They offer quality furniture made
more affordable. They are a
bonded company.

Gardens Past
P.O. Box 1846
Estes Park, CO 80517
Sent $1.00 for color catalog of
handmade, Rocky Mountain floral
art and herbal treasures.

The Gazebo of New York
127 East 57th St., Dept. CL
New York, NY 10022
$6 for catalog of large selection of
quilts, duvet covers, dust ruffles,
curtains, braided and rag rugs,
pillows, antique and new wicker,
and other hand-crafted accessories.

Gibson Interiors
417 S. Wrenn
High Point, NC 27260
(800) 247-5460
(910) 889-4939
Over 150 styles and 300 colors of
leather furniture featuring cost-plus
pricing. They also carry a full line of
lamps, mirrors, and all types of
accessories. Leather brands include:
Berkline, Emerson Leather, Glenncraft, Hickory International Design,

Interline Italia, Leather Trend, and Yorkshire. They offer shipping nation-wide.

Virginia Goodwin
Rt. 2, Box 770
Boone, NC 28607
(800) 735-5191
$1 for information on line of drapery, valances, canopies, bedspreads, and dust ruffles.

Golden Valley Lighting
274 Eastchester Dr.
High Point, NC 27260
(800) 735-3377
Up to 50 percent savings on lamps, fixtures, and accessories.

Graphik Dimensions LTD.
2103 Brentwood St.
High Point, NC 27263
(910) 887-3500
Save up to 70% off retail on ready-made picture frames, moldings, supplies, mirrors, and prints.

Holton Furniture Co.
P.O. Box 280
Thomasville, NC 27360
(800) 334-3183
Free information on furniture and accessories.

Home Decorator's Collection
2025 Concourse Dr.
St. Louis, MO 63146
(800) 245-2217
Free catalog of exterior accessories of all types, furniture, clock, lighting fixtures, bathroom accessories, and wicker.

House Dressing Furniture
3608 W. Wendover Ave.
Greensboro, NC 27407
(800) 322-5850
(910) 294-3900 NC residents

Discounted prices on furniture with international styling. Brands include: American Drew, Barcalounger, Bassett, Bob Timberlake, Childcraft, Chromecraft, Classic Gallery, Flexsteel, Henry Link, Hood, Hooker, Howard Miller, Kimball, Lane, Lexington, Lyon-Shaw, Madison Square, Nichols & Stone, Pulaski, Riverside, Stanley, Stanton-Cooper, Stratford, Stearns & Foster, Tell City, Tropitone, and Virginia House. Shipping available nationwide. Full line of interior furnishings represented. Special orders are welcome. Shipping available nationwide.

The House of Webster
P.O. Box BH 9102
Rogers, AR 72757
$1 for appliance folder and gift catalog. Modernized antique-reproduction appliances. 45 years of skilled craftsmanship.

Hubbardton Forge & Wood Corp.
P.O. Box 827
Castleton Corners
Castleton, VT 05735
(802) 468-3090
$3 for brochure of lamps, wrought-iron and brass chandeliers, pan racks, plant hangers, and bathroom acces-sories.

Hudson's Discount Furniture
P.O. Box 2547
Hickory, NC 28603
(704) 322-5717
Free information. Up to 50 percent savings on furniture and accessories.

Hutchins Furniture
P.O. Box 1427
Kemersville, NC 27285
(800) 334-2408
Free information on furniture and accessories.

IKEA, Inc.
P.O. Box 103016
Roswell, GA 30076-9860
(215) 834-0150
Check your yellow pages or call for
their nearest location and catalog.
This is a chain store offering Swedish-
style, reasonably-priced furniture,
lighting, flooring, and accessories.
Satisfaction guaranteed.

Interior Furnishings, LTD.
P.O. Box 1644
Hickory, NC 28603
(704) 328-5683
$3 for brochure. Up to 45 percent
savings on furniture and accessories.

Interiors of High Point
1701-C N. Main St.
High Point, NC 27262
(800) 999-0520
(910) 887-0520 NC residents
They specialize in home offices and
feature discounted office, contract
furnishings, home furnishings, outdoor
furnishings, Oriental rugs, pictures,
accessories. Over 300 lines represented, including: Flexsteel, Hekman,
Hickory-Fry, Hooker, Lane, Lexington,
Tropitone, and Universal. They offer
nationwide shipping.

John-Michael Furniture
2113 Hickory Blvd.
Hudson, NC 28638
Free information on a line of furniture and accessories. Lowest-possible
prices on name-brand furniture.

Kathryn's Collection
781 N. Main St.
High Point, NC 27260
Specializing in consignments, decorative accessories, antiques, and gifts
from showrooms, decorators and other
sellers.

Kemp & George
2515 E. 43rd St.
P.O. Box 182230
Chattanooga, TN 37422
(800) 562-1704
Free catalog offering lighting fixtures,
bathroom fixtures and accessories, and
other interior accessories.

Kimrick Decor
162 Eastern Ave.
Lynn, MA 01902
(617) 598-1400
$2 for catalog of accessories with the
following themes: nostalgia, Early
American, nautical, railroad, Western,
English pub, and Italian.

Kincaid Galleries
430 S. Main St.
High Point, NC 27260
(800) 883-1818
(910) 527-2570 NC residents
Large discounts on brand-name 18th-
century Shaker and traditional
furniture, wicker, recliners, bedding
and accessories. Custom upholstery
available. Brands include: Barcalounger, Custom Upholstery, Lane,
Lloyd/Flanders, and Serta. Shipping
available nationwide.

Knight Gallery
P.O. Box 1254
Lenoir, NC 28645
(800) 334-4721
Free information on a line of furniture
and accessories.

Thomas H. Kramer, Inc.
805 Depot St.
Commerce Park
Columbus, IN 47201
(812) 379-4097
$3 for catalog of period and country-
styled furniture and accessories.

The Lamp Shop
4221 Garrett Rd.
Durham, NC
(919) 493-0661
Save 10 to 60% off retail on in-stock
lamps. Over 350 styles to choose from.
Framed prints are 20% off retail.

LeFort Furniture
293 Winter St.
Hanover, MA 02339
(617) 826-9033
$6 for portfolio of furniture and
accessories.

The Linen Source
5401 Hangar Court
Tampa, FL 33631-3151
(800) 431-2620
Call for a free catalog. Discounted
bedroom ensembles, curtains, accessories, and rugs. Satisfaction
guaranteed.

Loftin-Black Furniture Co.
111 Sedgehill Dr.
Thomasville, NC 27360
(800) 334-7398
(919) 472-6117 NC residents
or
214 N. Main St.
High Point, NC 27262
(910) 883-4711
Send SASE for free information on
over 300 major brands of furniture
and accessories at discounted prices.
Featuring bedroom, dining room,
occasional, upholstered, bedding
lamps, accessories, and pictures.
Nationwide home delivery. Business
established 1948.

Magnolia Hall
726 Andover
Atlanta, GA 30327
$3 for 80-page catalog of
assortment of furniture. Huge
selection of sofas, beds, carved

furniture, chairs, tables, lamps,
clocks, mirrors, and desks.

The Marble Shop
100 Bliss Ave.
Pittsburg, CA 94565
They offer an assortment of marble
products.

Marble Technics
150 E. 58th St.
New York, NY 10022
Send for information on their line
of decorative marble products.

Mathews Wire
654 W. Morrison St.
Frankfort, IN 46041
(317) 659-3542
Free information on wire and wood
decorative country accessories.

Mecklenburg Furniture Shops
520 Providence Rd.
Charlotte, NC 28207
(704) 333-5891
Free brochure of available furniture
and accessories.

Mills River
713 Old Orchard Rd.
Hendersonville, NC 28739
(800) 874-4898
$2 for catalog of flat-braided rugs, bird
houses, and holiday decorative accessories.

Montgomery Ward Direct
(800) 852-2711
Call for a free catalog featuring
discounted prices on bedding and bath
ensembles, bedspreads, accessories,
curtains, rugs, bedroom, living and
family room furniture.

Muckleberry Farms
1240 Lynway Ln.
Atlanta, GA 30311

$3 for catalog featuring country quilts, wreaths, and accessories.

Museum of Modern Art, New York
Mail-Order Dept.
P.O. Box 2534
West Chester, PA 19380
(212) 708-9888
$3 for catalog of modern accessories for home and office.

Oak-Wood Furniture Galleries, Inc.
3800 Comanche Rd.
Archdale, NC 27263
(910) 431-9126
Save up to 80% off retail on name-brand American manufactured furniture, including upholstery, bedroom, dining room, entertainment centers, and accessories. Brands include: American Drew, Bassett, Howard Miller Clocks, Lexington, Pulaski, Ridgeway, and Singer. Much of the furniture is in stock. Offering nationwide shipping.

Olde Mill House Shoppe
105 Strasburg Pike
Lancaster, PA 17602
(717) 299-0678
$1 for catalog offering country-styled furniture, bathroom accessories, linens, braided rugs.

The Old Wagon Factory
P.O. Box 1427, Dept. CL14
Clarksville, VA 23927
(804) 374-5787
$2 for catalog of available Chippendale furniture, Victorian porch furniture, railings and trim, planters and benchs, home and garden accessories, wooden storm-screen doors, hardware.

Panorama Wood Products
P.O. Box 250
Kettle Falls, WA 99141

(800) 227-6352
$2 for color brochure of solid pine country collectibles for your home.

Parkway Furniture Galleries
Hwy. 105 South
P.O. Box 2450
Boone, NC 28607
(704) 264-3993
Free information on furniture and accessories.

Pennsylvania House Collectors' Gallery of High Point
P.O. Box 6437
1300 North Main St.
High Point, NC 27262
Mailing address:
P.O. Box 6437
High Point, NC 27262
(910) 887-3000
Clearance center with discounts of up to 50% on living-room, bedroom, dining-room, upholstery, leather furniture, bedding, rugs, entertainment units, lamps, and accessories. Pennsylvania House and other interior furnishings. They ship nationwide.

Pier 1 Imports
(800) 447-4371, call for the store nearest you. Chain store that carries imported furniture and accessories from all over the world.

Plexi-Craft Quality Products Corporation
514 W. 24th St.
New York, NY 10011
(800) 24-PLEXI, (212) 924-3244
$2 for 16-page catalog of lucite and plexiglass furniture and accessories. From small bathroom accessories and fixtures to television stands.

The Pottery Barn
P.O. Box 7044
San Francisco, CA 94120-7044

(415) 421-3400
Call or write for catalog. A range of home accessories. Satisfaction guaranteed. Business established 44 years ago.

Priba Furniture Sales & Interiors
210 Stage Coach Trail
Greensboro, NC 27409
Mailing address:
P.O. Box 13295
Greensboro, NC 27415
Free information. Up to 45 percent savings on furniture, lighting, and accessories from over 250 major manufacturers. Brands include: Bernhardt, Broyhill, Chapman Classic Leather, Distinction Leather, Hickory Chair, Hekman, Hickory-White, Hooker, Karges, LaBarge, Lane, Leathercraft, Lenox Lighting, Lexington, Stanley, Stanton-Cooper, Statton, Thomasville, Vanguard, and Woodmark. Shipping available nationwide.

Quality Furniture Market of Lenoir, Inc.
2034 Hickory Blvd., S.W.
Lenoir, NC 28645
Send for information on discounted furniture, bedding, linens, accessories, and lampshades.

The Renovator's Supply
Renovator's Old Mill
Millers Falls, MA 01349
(413) 659-2211
$3 for catalog of reproduction antique hardware, lighting, rugs, bathroom and plumbing fixtures, accessories, and curtains.

Rose & Gerard
55 Sunnyside
Mill Valley, CA 94941
Free catalog of dining dishes and miscellaneous accessories, pottery,

lanterns, Dhurrie rugs, basketry, candles, and plant stands.

Sante Fe Country
1218 King St.
Alexandria, VA 22314
(800) 257-9577
Free catalog of Sante Fe country accessories, gifts, and furniture.

Shaw Furniture Galleries Clearance Center
South Main at College Dr.
High Point, NC
(910) 889-4889
Retail Showroom
P.O. Box 576
Randleman, NC 27317
(919) 498-2628
Free information on 300 lines of furniture and accessories with savings of up to 40 percent off retail. Featuring order cancellations, showroom samples, and factory closeouts. Brands include: Bassett, Bernhardt, Broyhill, Carsons, Classic Leather, Hickory Chair, Hickory-White, and Thomasville. Nationwide delivery and setup. Business established in 1940.

W.L. Smith Co.
RFD 1 Rt.4
Epsom, NH 03234
They offer a line of copper weathervanes and lanterns.

Spiegel Catalog
P.O. Box 6340
Chicago, IL 60680-6340
(800) 345-4500
$3 for catalog featuring a full range of interior products, furniture, curtains, draperies, accessories, rugs, lamps, etc. Many items discounted or available discounted through subsequent sale catalogs. Satisfaction guaranteed.

St. Charles Furniture
P.O. Box 2144
High Point, NC 27261
(800) 545-3287
Free information on available
furniture and accessories.

Sturbridge Yankee Workshop
Blueberry Rd.
Westbrook, ME 04092
Send for catalog of traditional repro-
duction furniture and accessories.

Sutton-Council Furniture
P.O. Box 3288
Wilmington, NC 28406
(919) 799-1990
$5 for catalog featuring furniture and
accessories.

Thomas Home Furnishings, Inc.
4346 Hickory Blvd.
Granite Falls, NC 28630
(704) 396-2147
Discounted prices on furniture for
living rooms, dining rooms, offices,
outdoors, bedding, and accessories.
Brands include: American Drew,
Century, Clayton Marcus, Councill,
Knob Creek, La-Z-Boy, Leathercraft,
Lexington, Serta, Stanley, and
Wellington Hall. Shipping available
nationwide.

Touch of Class
Order Dept.
1905 N. Van Buren St.
Huntingburg, IN 47542
(800) 457-7456
Free catalog offering bedroom and
bathroom ensembles, including bedspreads, curtains, drapery, and fabric
accessories, bathroom accessories,
lamps, and miscellaneous related
accessories.

Tysinger's Antiques
609 National Hwy.

Thomasville, NC 27361
(910) 883-4477
Direct importers of fine antiques from
England and France. Also available at
this location; decorative accessories,
art, and fine reproduction furniture
from the 18th and 19th centuries,
including: Baker, Kittinger, Tomlinson,
and John Widdicomb. Business
established 1959.

Utility Craft
2630 Eastchester Dr.
High Point, NC 27265
(910) 454-6153
Solid-wood 18th-century and traditional furniture and furnishings.
Including bedroom, dining room,
upholstery, leather, lamps, and
accessories. Catalog sales available.
Major brands include: American
Drew, LaBarge, La-Z-Boy, Hekman,
Lexington, Nichols & Stone, Pennsylvania Classics, Stanley, Stanton-
Cooper, Statton, and Waterford. They
ship and setup nationwide. Business
established in 1949.

Lillian Vernon
Virginia Beach, VA 23479-0002
(914) 633-6300
Free catalog on a range of accessories.
Satisfaction Guaranteed.

Victorian Country Candles
(800) 843-6324
Free brochure. They are manufacturers of quality scented
candles.

Victorian Sampler
P.O. Box 344
Mt. Morris, IL 61054-7930
(708) 377-8000 for subscriptions.
This is a magazine that is available at
bookstores and grocery stores for $4
per copy and is filled with Victorian

decorative accessories from a nationwide network of artistans and crafters
who ship directly to you.

Allan Walker Ltd.
3800 Ivy Rd., NE
Atlanta, GA 30305
(404) 233-1926
Free information on line of imported
tapestries.

**Warren's Interior Design & Furniture,
Inc.**
P.O. Box 33
Prospect Hill, NC 27314
(800) 743-9792
(910) 562-5198 NC residents
Up to 60% off retail on furniture
from the following brands: Bassett,
Clayton Marcus, Flexsteel, Henry-
Link, Hooker, Leathercraft, Link-
Taylor, Sealy Mattresses, White, and
Howard Miller Clocks. Carpet brands
include: Cabin Crafts, Masland,
Philadelphia, and Sun. Fabric and
wallpaper brands include: Greeff,
Payne, and Schumacher. They also
have a large selection of pictures and
accessories.

Wicker Warehouse
195 S. River St.
Hackensack, NJ 07601
(800) 274-8602
(201) 342-6709 for NJ residents
Call for catalog on wicker furniture
and accessories.

Martha Wetherbee
P.O. Box 116
Sanbornton, NH 03269
(603) 286-8927
$3 for 28-page catalog of baskets.

Wild Wings
South Hwy. 61
Lake City, MN 55041
(800) 445-4833

Featuring furnishings and accessories
with a wildlife theme.

Wild Wood Gallery
502 Factory Ave.
P.O. Box 300
Syracuse, NY 13205
(315) 454-8098
They offer a line of pictures and
mirrors.

Windrift Furniture Gallery
145 Industrial Ave.
Greensboro, NC 27406
(919) 379-8895
Free information. Up to 40 percent
savings on furniture and accessories.

Yield House
P.O. Box 5000
North Conway, NH 03860
(800) 258-4720
Free information on country furniture,
curtains, accessories, and collectibles.

Young's Furniture and Rug Company
1706 N. Main St.
P.O. Box 5005
High Point, NC 27262
(910) 883-4111
Large discounts on major lines of fine
furniture, including: Century, Councill,
Hancock & Moore, Henredon, Hick-
ory Chair, John Widdicomb, Karges,
Lexington, Maitland-Smith, and
Wright Table. Also includes uphol-
stery, leather, accessories, and lamps.
Business established 1946.

Historic Hardware and Fixtures

Antique Hardware Store
9718 Easton Rd., Rt. 611
Kintersville, PA 18930
(800) 422-9982
$3 for catalog of reproduction tin and
wood chandeliers, interior and exterior
lamps, fixtures, hardware, pedestal
sinks, and high-tank toilets.

Baldwin Hardware Corp.
841 E. Wyomissing Blvd.
P.O. Box 15048
Reading, PA 19612
$3 for catalog of lighting fixtures. $.75
for brochure featuring bathroom
accessories, $.75 for brochure
featuring door hardware, $.75 for
brochure featuring decorative
hardware.

Barap Specialties
835 Bellows Ave.
Frankfort, MI 49635
(616) 352-9863
$1 for catalog of lamp parts, chair-
caning supplies, turned-wood parts,
etc.

Charolette Ford Trunks
P.O. Box 536
Spearman, TX 79081
(800) 553-2649
$3 for catalog of antique-trunk
repair supplies. $4 for Trunk I.D.
Guide. $6.50 for Trunk Talk (24
pages of photos, ideas, and
instructions on restoring all styles of
trunks).

Decorum
235-237 Commercial St.
Portland, ME 04101
(207) 775-3346
Free information on their line of
roll-top desks, file cabinets, antique
lamps, bathroom and plumbing

fixtures, and hardware.

Historic Housefitters
Dept. 1014
Farm to Market Rd.
Brewster, NY 10509
(914) 278-2427
$3 for 48-page catalog. The
sourcebook of 18th-century quality
period hardware and lighting. Handmade light fixtures, brass, procelain
and leaded crystal door knobs, lever
sets, etc.

Horton Brasses
Nooks Hill Rd./P.O. Box 120
Cromwell, CT 06416
(203) 635-4400
$3 for catalog. Manufacturers of
antique furniture hardware for over 50
years.

Pintchik Homeworks
2106 Bath Ave.
Brooklyn, NY 11214
(800) 847-4199
(718) 996-5580 NY residents
Free brochure and order kit for
wallpaper, window-treatment hardware
and supplies, paint, and floorcoverings.
They guarantee the lowest prices.
Business established in 1912.

Reggio Register
P.O. Box 511, Dept.L 308
Ayer, MA 01432
$1 for catalog of grilles and
registers made of cast iron and cast
brass.

The Renovator's Supply
Renovator's Old Mill
Millers Falls, MA 01349
(413) 659-2211
$3 for catalog of reproduced
antique hardware, lighting, rugs,

bathroom and plumbing fixtures,
accessories, and curtains.

Rufkahr's
4207 Eagle Rock Ct.
St Charles, MO 63304
$2 for 77-page catalog of
reproduction antique hardware.

Architectural Details

Classic Doors & Mantels
2100 S. Main St.
High Point, NC 27263
(910) 889-3667
or
1-C 2810 Yonkers
Raleigh, NC 27613
(919) 829-0208
Brochures available. Factory-direct
prices on sofas, loveseats, sleepers,
chairs, ottomans, and chaise lounges.
Up to 60% off retail. Selection of over
500 fabrics. Handcrafted doors and
fireplace mantles. Custom-made to
your specifications. Worldwide
shipping available.

Graphik Dimensions LTD.
2103 Brentwood St.
High Point, NC 27263
(910) 887-3500
Save up to 70% off retail on ready-
made picture frames, moldings,
supplies, mirrors, and prints.

The Old Wagon Factory
P.O. Box 1427, Dept. CL14
Clarksville, VA 23927
(804) 374-5787
$2 for catalog of Victorian porch
furniture and trim, planters and
benchs, home and garden accessories,
and wooden storm-screen doors.

Readybuilt Products Co.
P.O. Box 4425
Baltimore, MD 21223-0425
Send for information on their line of
wood mantles.

**Uncle John's Gingerbread House
Trim**
5229 Choupique Rd.
Sulphur, LA 70663
$2 for catalog of economically-priced
brackets, pendants, and gables in

matching sets.

Vintage Wood Works
Hwy. 34 South
P.O. Box R #2420
Quinlan, TX 75474
(903) 356-2158
$2 for catalog (includes how-to ideas)
of solid-wood reproductions for interiors and exteriors. Spandrels, shelves,
window cornices, porch and newel
posts, balusters, mouldings, gables,
brackets, corbels, screen doors, etc.
Satisfaction guaranteed.

Appliance Reproductions

Country Accents
P.O. Box 437
Montoursville, PA 17754
(717) 478-4127
$5 for 80-page color catalog of
country-styled, handcrafted, pierced-
metal panels for kitchen cabinets,
appliances, etc. Standard or custom-
made sizes in fourteen different
finishes. Established in 1979.

The House of Webster
P.O. Box BH 9102
Rogers, AR 72757
$1 for appliance folder and gift
catalog. Modernized antique repro-
uctions of appliances. 45 years
of skilled craftmanship.

Lehman's
P.O. Box 41, Dept. 1-TDB
Kidron, OH 44636
$2 for 2,000-item Amish catalog.
Traditional heartland cookstoves
(woodfired, gas or electric), grain mills,
oil lamps, cast cookware, crockery and
other Amish accessories.

Wood Stoves

Ashley Heater Co.
P.O. Box 128
Florence, AL 35630
Send for information. Manufacturer of
woodstoves and fireplaces.

Olde Towne Chimney Sweeps
1123 Kentucky St.
Racine, WI 53405
(800) 886-4568
$2 for catalog of woodstoves, acces-
sories, equipment, etc. 100 percent
guaranteed.

Vulcan Stove Co.
P.O. Box 696
Louisville KY 20201
They offer an assortment of all types
of stoves.

Woodstock Soapstone Co., Inc.
66 Airpark Rd.
West Lebanon, NH 03784
(800) 866-4344
Free information on high-efficiency
soapstone stoves.

Professional Organizations and Associations

Professional organizations and associations will provide you with a wealth of information and publications if you write or call them and request it. Call 800 directory assistance (1-800-555-1212) and inquire if the organization or association you wish to call has added an 800 number, if one isn't already listed.

Allied Board of Trade
555 Mamaroneck Ave.
Harrison, NY 10528
(212) 473-3877

American Association of Wholesale Showrooms
P.O. Box 218
Beverly Hills, CA 90213
(213) 936-1414

American Canvas Institute
10 Beach St.
Berea, OH 44017

American Furniture Manufacturers Association
P.O. Box HP-7
High Point, NC 27261
(919) 884-5000

American Hardware Manufacturers Association
931 N. Plum Grove Rd.
Schaumburg, IL 60173-4796
(708) 605-1025

American Institute of Architects (AIA)*
1130 Connecticut N.W., Ste. 625
Washington, DC 20036
(202) 828-0993
* Professional organization for registered architects

American Lighting Association
435 North Michigan Ave.
#1717
Chicago, IL 60611
(312) 644-0828

American Parquet Association
2900 First Commercial Building
Little Rock, AR 72201

American Society for Testing & Materials
1916 Race
Philadelphia, PA 19103
(215) 299-5400

American Society of Furniture Designers (ASFD)*
521 Hamilton
High Point, NC 27261
(919) 884-4074
* Professional organization for furniture designers

American Society of Interior Designers (ASID)*
608 Massachusetts Ave. N.E.
Washington, DC 20002
(202) 546-3480
* Worldwide professional organization for interior designers

American Society of Landscape Designers (ASLA)*
4401 Connecticut Ave., N.W.
Washington, DC 20008
(202) 686-2752
* Professional organization for landscape designers

American Textile Manufacturers Institute
1801 K St N.W., Ste 900
Washington, D.C. 20006
(202) 862-0552

American Window Covering Manufacturers Association (AWCMA)*
355 Lexington Ave.
New York, NY 10017
(212) 661-4261
* Represents leading mfg./suppliers of hard window coverings

**Architectural Woodwork
Institute**
2310 South Walter Reed Dr.
Arlington, VA 22206
(703) 671-9100

**Art & Antique Dealers'
League of America**
1020 Madison Ave.
New York, NY 10006
(212) 879-7558

**Art Deco Society of Los
Angeles**
P.O. Box 972
Hollywood, CA 90078
(213) 659-DECO

**Art Deco Society of New
York**
90 West St.
New York, NY 10006
(212) 925-4946

**Associated Landscape
Contractors of America***
405 North Washington St.
Falls Church, VA 22046
(703) 241-4004
* Association of landscape
contractors

**Association of Registered
Interior Designers of Ontario**
168 N Bedford Rd.
Toronto, ON M5R 2K9
(416) 921-2127

**Association of University
Interior Designers**
Miami University
Cook Place
Oxford, OH 45056
(513) 529-3730

**Better Fabric Testing
Bureau, Inc.**
101 West 31st. St.
New York, NY 10001
(212) 868-7090

**Business & Institutional
Furniture Manufacturers'
Association (BIFMA)**
2335 Burton, S.E.
Grand Rapids, MI 49506
(616) 243-1681

**California Redwood
Association**
405 Enfrente Dr.,#200
Novato, CA 94949
(415) 382-0662

**The Carpet and
Rug Institute***
P.O. Box 2048
Dalton, GA 30722
(706) 278-3176
(404) 278-3176
(202) 429-6629
* National trade association for the carpet-
and-rug industry

**Carpet Manufacturers'
Association of the West**
100 North Citrus St., #235
West Covina, CA 91791
(818) 967-5268

Center for Fire Research
National Institute of
Standards & Technology
A247 Polymers Bldg.
Gaithersburg, MD 20899
(301) 975-6850

Ceramic Tile Institute
700 North Virgil Ave.
Los Angeles, CA 90029
(213) 660-1911

**Color Association of
the United States***
409 W. 44th St.
New York, NY 10036
(212) 582-6884
* Publisher of annual color forecast for
interior colors

The Color Marketing Group (CMG)*
4001 N. 9th St., Ste. 102
Arlington, VA 22203
(703) 528-7666

* A professional organization that forecasts colors two years ahead

Contract Furnishings Council*
1190 Merchandise Mart
Chicago, IL 60654
(312) 321-0563
* Full-service contract dealer association

Cultured-Marble Institute
435 North Michigan Ave.
Chicago, IL 60611
(312) 644-0828

Decorative Laminate-Products Association
600 S. Federal, Ste. 400
Chicago, IL 60605

Decorative Window-Coverings Association (DWCA)*
1050 N. Lindbergh Blvd.
St. Louis, MO 63132-2994
(314) 991-3470
* Non-profit association of fabricators/distributors

Design International
3748 22nd St.
San Francisco, CA 94114
(415) 647-4700

Designers' Saturday, Inc.*
A & D Building
150 E. 58th St.
New York, NY 10155
(212) 826-3155
* Trade association of New York contract and residential-furnishing firms

Drapery Manufacturers' Association of California*
P.O. Box 6611
Orange, CA 92665
(714) 636-7382
* California association of drapery manufacturers

Formica Corporation
Information Center
114 Mayfield St.

Edison, NJ 08837

The Foundation for Interior Design Education Research (FIDER)*
60 Monroe Center, N.W.
Grand Rapids, MI 49503
(616) 458-0400
* Accredits interior-design programs in U.S. and Canada

Home Fashion Information Network*
557 S. Duncan
Clearwater, FL 34616
(813) 443-2702
(800) 875-9255
* Publishes and distributes information to the wall coverings industry

Home Fashion Products Association (HFPA)*
355 Lexington Ave.
New York, NY 10017-6603
(212) 661-4261
* Professional organization of manufacturers/suppliers of soft window treatments and home furnishings

Illuminating Engineering Society of North America
345 East 47th St.
New York, NY 10017
(212) 705-7926

Indian Arts and Crafts Association
4215 Lead, S.E.
Albuquerque, NM 87018
(505) 265-9149

Industrial Designers Society of America
1142-E Walker Rd.
Great Falls, VA 22066
(703) 759-0100

Institute of Business Designers (IBD)*
341 Merchandise Mart
Chicago, IL 60654
(312) 467-1950

* Contract interior designers' professional association

Institute of Store Designers
25 North Broadway
Tarrytown, NY 10591
(914) 332-1806

Interior Design Educator Council (IDEC)
14252 Culver Dr.
Irvine, CA 92714
(312) 467-1950

Interior Designers of Canada (IDC)
160 Pears Ave.
Toronto, Ontario
CAN M5R ITZ

Interior Plantscape Association
11800 Sunrise Valley Dr.
Reston, VA 22091
(703) 771-7044

International Association of Lighting Designers
18 East 16th St.
New York, NY 10003
(212) 206-1281

International Furnishings and Design Association (IFDA)*
107 World Trade Center
P.O. Box 58045
Dallas, TX 75258
(214) 747-2406
* Non-profit organization that promotes interior-design education and networking among leaders in the industry

International Linen Promotion Commission
200 Lexington Ave. #225
New York, NY 10016
(212) 685-0424

International Society of Interior Designers (ISID)*
433 S. Spring St., Ste. 6-D
Los Angeles, CA 90013

(213) 680-4240
* Educational organization for interior designers and members of the trade

Italian Tile Council
499 Park Ave.
New York, NY 10022

Laminate Council of America
P.O. Box 725
Mahwah, NJ 07430

Marble Institute of America
33505 State St.
Farmington, MI 48335
(313) 476-5558

National Art-Dealer Association
5669 Friendship Station
Washington, DC 20016
(202) 537-1000

National Association of Display Industries
470 Park Ave. S.
New York, NY 10016
(212) 213-2662

National Association of Store-Fixture Manufacturers
5975 West Sunrise Blvd.
Sunrise, FL 33313
(305) 587-9190

National Council on Interior-Design Qualification (NCIDQ)
118 E. 25th St.
New York, NY 10010
(212) 473-1199

National Decorating-Products Association (NDPA)*
1050 N. Lindbergh Blvd.
St. Louis, MO 63132
(314) 991-3470
* Trade association for retailers of decorative products

National Fire Protection Association
Batterymarch Park
Quincy, MA 02269

(617) 770-3000

**National Home
Fashion League**
107 World Trade Center
Dallas, TX 75207
(214) 747-2406

**National Kitchen-and-
Bath Association**
124 Main St.
Hackettstown, NJ 07840
(201) 852-0033

**National Institute of
Governmental Purchasing**
115 Hillwood Ave.
Falls Church, VA 22046
(703) 533-7300

**National Oak Flooring
Manufacturing Association
Oak Flooring Institute***
P.O. Box 3009
Memphis, TN 38173
(901) 526-5016
* Trade association for flooring
manufacturers

**National Office-Products
Association (NOPA)**
301 N. Fairfax St.
Alexandria, VA 22314
(703) 549-9040

**National Paint-and-
Coatings Association**
1500 Rhode Island Ave., N.W.
Washington, DC 20001
(202) 462-6272

**National Restaurant
Association**
1200 17th St., N. W.
Washington, DC 20036
(202) 331-5900

**National Trust for Historic
Preservation**
1785 Massachusetts Ave., N.W.
Washington, DC 20036
(202) 673-4000

**National Wholesale-
Furniture Association**
209 South Main St., #M-1412
High Point, NC 27261
(919) 889-6411

Professional Picture-Framers' Association
P.O. Box 7655
Richmond, VA 23231
(804) 226-0430

**Resilient Floor Covering
Institute***
966 Hungerford Dr., Ste. 12-B
Rockville, MD 20850
(301) 340-8580
* Trade association for manufacturers of
resilient tile & sheet-vinyl products

Resource Council Inc.
979 Third Ave., #902N
New York, NY 10022
(212) 752-9040

**Sealed Insulating-Glass
Manufacturers' Association**
11 E. Wacker Dr., Ste.600
Chicago, IL 60601

**Society for Marketing
Professional Services**
99 Canal Center Plaza
Alexandria, VA 22314
(703) 549-6117

**The Society of Environmental
Graphic Designers**
47 Third St.
Cambridge, MA 02141
(617) 577-8225

Stevens' Linen Association
P.O. Box 220
Webster, MA 01570

Tile Council of America
P.O. Box 326
Princeton, NJ 08542-0326
(609) 921-7050

**Upholstered-Furniture Action
Council (UFAC)**
P.O. Box 2436

High Point, NC 27261
(919) 885-5065

**Wall-Upholstery Guild
of America**
201 E. 28th St.
New York, NY 10016
(212) 532-2449

Wallcovering Association (WMA)*
355 Lexington Ave.
New York, NY 10016
(312) 644-6610
* Wallcovering association for
manufacturers and distributors

**Wallcovering Information
Bureau**
66 Morris Ave.
Springfield, NJ 07081
(201) 379-1100

**Western-Wood Products
Association**
1500 Yeon Building
Portland, OR 97204

**Window-Coverings
Association of America (WCAA)***
1050 N. Lindbergh Blvd.
St. Louis, MO 63132
(314) 997-0558
* Window covering retailers' trade
association

**Wood Moulding & Millwork
Producers Association**
1730 S.W. Skyline Blvd.
P.O. Box 25278
Portland, OR 97225
(503) 292-9288

The Wool Bureau*
360 Lexington Ave.
New York, NY 10017
(212) 986-6222
* Non-profit organization
engaged in promoting wool products

Index

Books Published by *Touch of Design* ®

Secrets of Success for Today's Interior Designers and Decorators
Easily Sell the Job, Plan It Correctly, and Keep Your Clients Coming Back

This book provides a <u>wealth</u> of knowledge, experience, and benefits for *all* interior designers and decorators. Your guide to accurate planning, measuring and selling the job, whether you are new to the ID field or are very practiced, *everyone* gains knowledge and experience from this book. Improve your sales ability, design planning/measuring skills, and fabric selection expertise. Determine what will and won't work for the specific situation and gain an overall increased knowledge in the ID field. The realm of alternate and fabric window treatments is thoroughly covered. Follow the advice, use the information, and become a window treatment expert.

Complete explanations and extensive professional advice are included. Learn methods for getting better leads, proven marketing and advertising techniques, how to eliminate your competition, and how to be financially successful *today* in this career. Buy this book <u>now</u> if you want to *increase* your sales and profits and eliminate problems. **You get a reference packed with information to ensure your success. 336 pgs. (8 ½" x 11"). SATISFACTION GUARANTEED!** Written by Linda M. Ramsay.

Start Your Own Interior Design Business and Keep It Growing!
Your Guide to Business Success

You'll find a complete and lucrative business plan covering *everything* you need to know from A to Z to start and grow a successful interior design business. There are many more Touch of Design® prospecting, marketing, and advertising secrets. Don't start an ID business without *this* book. This is *your* guide to business success. This book is *filled* with successful, useful, practical, helpful, and profitable ideas for anyone starting or attempting to grow an interior-design business. A <u>must</u> for interior-design businesses just starting up — *but* should be read by *all* interior design business owners who want to prosper and flourish and earn more money in today's business climate. *All* will benefit from this new book. <u>**Extremely comprehensive and complete.**</u> **384 pgs. (8½" x 11").** Written by Linda M. Ramsay.

The NEW 1994 Fabric Cross-Reference Source
<u>The NATIONAL APPLE CHART</u>

This expanded and updated decorative fabric reference source includes 75,000 cross-referenced fabrics from 95 vendors/jobbers, and over 30 mills!! Don't try and sell fabrics without this reference book! *It solves your fabric availability problems.* Save fabric backorders, lost orders, time, stress, frustration and money! This is <u>your</u> cross-reference guide to finding required fabrics from other sources. This is a vital and necessary tool for your use. *Just <u>one</u> saved order will more than pay for this tool. Find an alternative fabric source* instead of <u>spending more time</u> reselecting and reselling another fabric for the job. Written by Bill Peacock.

Successful Window Dressing and Interior Design

Your Guide to Achieving Excellent Results!

Consumers guide to creating successful interiors. Included are the extensive window planning and measuring sections, and fabric details from _Secrets of Success for Today's Interior Designers and Decorators_ and directories from _Start Your Own Interior Design Business and Keep It Growing!_ How to make correct selections, avoid mistakes and problems, find and work with superior designers if you don't want to do it yourself, get the most for your money, find your style, achieve custom results, select what is right for your home, situation, personality, and budget, cut the price down, get the best possible pricing, work with existing furnishings, measure, plan, and determine yardage for all types of window and fabric accessories, make effective fabric selections, determine what will and won't work are all included. Written by Linda M. Ramsay.

Interior-Design-Furnishings Directory of Discounted 800-Number and Hard-to-Find Companies

Insider's Home Decorating Guide to Lower-Priced and Little-Known Companies that Offer You <u>Substantial Savings</u> and <u>Higher Values</u>

If you are interested in buying goods less expensively, whether you are a designer, decorator, or a consumer attempting to stretch your decorating dollars further, this is the interior-goods resource book for you. Includes hard-to-find sources that offer quality goods with lower prices. Designers will be surprised to find how to get better prices through these companies than through their regular sources. You get many sources for mini and wood blinds, vertical blinds, Duettes, pleated and roller shades; drapery rods and hardware; drapery, curtains, valances, bedspreads, quilts, linens, and fabric accessories; fabrics; art; carpeting and rugs, wood flooring, marble, resilient floorcoverings; wallcoverings; furniture; lighting and lamps; lamp shades; accessories, clocks, and collectibles; outdoor furnishings and garden accessories; historic hardware and fixtures; office furniture and accessories; stencilling; table pads; architectural details; appliance reproductions, and wood stoves. Written by Linda M. Ramsay.

Interior Design Computer Bulletin Board

Touch of Design ®
475 College Blvd., Ste. 6290
Oceanside, CA 92057
(619) 945-4283 bulletin board accessable via computer modem
(619) 945-7909 voice

We are setting up a computer bulletin board (BBS) for designers, decorators and consumers of interior design to address problems, concerns, resources, etc. Everyone who calls can access the questions and the answers and participate. Our interior-design book catalog and reports will be online and available to download, free. Our internet email address is: todesign@cyber.net.

Ordering Information

These books are <u>filled</u> with details to ensure your success and are <u>real values</u>.

Yes, I am interested in investing in my future. Please send me:

- *Secrets of Success for Today's Interior Designers and Decorators* $39.99_____

- *Start Your Own Interior Design Business and Keep It Growing!* 39.99_____

- *The NATIONAL APPLE CHART* 39.99_____

- *Successful Window Dressing and Interior Design* 24.99_____

- *Interior Design-Furnishings Directory of Discounted 800-Number*.......19.99_____

California residents add sales tax — 7½%_____

Shipping/handling: one book $3.45, $1.50 for each additional book _____

Total_____

- **Need more information or volume rates?**
  Write or call us at (619) 945-7909.

Only prepaid orders will be accepted. Checks, money orders, Visa, and Mastercard may be used for ordering.

Name/Firm_____Address_____

City_____State_____Zip_____

Signature_____Card Number_____

Credit card expiration date _____

Phone Number_____

Type of credit card: ☐ Visa ☐ Mastercard

Mail to: *Touch of Design*®

475 College Blvd., Ste. 6290, Oceanside, CA 92057

Are you on our mailing list? If you did not purchase this book directly from Touch of Design, send us your name and address for future available books by Touch of Design®.

Please tell your friends and associates in the interior-design field about these books.

Photocopy this page — Retain for Future Reference!

Ordering Information

These books are <u>filled</u> with details to ensure your success and are <u>real values</u>.

Yes, I am interested in investing in my future. Please send me:

- *Secrets of Success for Today's Interior Designers and Decorators* $39.99_____

- *Start Your Own Interior Design Business and Keep It Growing!*   39.99_____

- *The NATIONAL APPLE CHART*   39.99_____

- *Successful Window Dressing and Interior Design*   24.99_____

- *Interior Design-Furnishings Directory of Discounted 800-Number*.......19.99_____

California residents add sales tax — 7½%_____

Shipping/handling: one book $3.45, $1.50 for each additional book   _____

Total_____

- **Need more information or volume rates?**
  Write or call us at (619) 945-7909.

Only prepaid orders will be accepted. Checks, money orders, Visa, and Mastercard may be used for ordering.

Name/Firm_____Address_____

City_____State_____Zip_____

Signature_____Card Number_____

Credit card expiration date _____

Phone Number_____

Type of credit card: ☐ Visa   ☐ Mastercard

Mail to: *Touch of Design*®

475 College Blvd., Ste. 6290, Oceanside, CA 92057

Are you on our mailing list? If you did not purchase this book directly from Touch of Design, send us your name and address for future available books by Touch of Design®.

Please tell your friends and associates in the interior-design field about these books.

Photocopy this page — Retain for Future Reference!

Ordering Information

These books are __filled__ with details to ensure your success and are __real values__.

Yes, I am interested in investing in my future. Please send me:

- *Secrets of Success for Today's Interior Designers and Decorators* $39.99_____

- *Start Your Own Interior Design Business and Keep It Growing!*   **39.99**_____

- *The NATIONAL APPLE CHART*   **39.99**_____

- *Successful Window Dressing and Interior Design*   **24.99**_____

- *Interior Design-Furnishings Directory of Discounted 800-Number*.......19.99_____

California residents add sales tax — 7½%_____

Shipping/handling: one book $3.45, $1.50 for each additional book   _____

Total_____

- **Need more information or volume rates?**
  Write or call us at (619) 945-7909.

Only prepaid orders will be accepted. Checks, money orders, Visa, and Mastercard may be used for ordering.

Name/Firm_____Address_____

City_____State_____Zip_____

Signature_____Card Number_____

Credit card expiration date _____

Phone Number_____

Type of credit card: ☐ Visa   ☐ Mastercard

Mail to: *Touch of Design*®

475 College Blvd., Ste. 6290, Oceanside, CA 92057

Are you on our mailing list? If you did not purchase this book directly from Touch of Design, send us your name and address for future available books by Touch of Design®.

Please tell your friends and associates in the interior-design field about these books.

Photocopy this page — Retain for Future Reference!